REPRESENTATIVE MEN

Representative Men

In the Light of Anthroposophy

Moses • Grünewald • Goethe • Nietzsche
Wilde • Kafka • Eckstein • Steiner

T. H. Meyer

2012
Lindisfarne Books

2012
LINDISFARNE BOOKS
An imprint of SteinerBooks / Anthroposophic Press, Inc.
610 Main Street, Great Barrington, MA 01230
www.steinerbooks.org

Copyright © 2012 by T. H. Meyer
and Perseus Verlag Basel (www.perseus.ch)

All rights reserved. No part of this book may be reproduced, stored in a retrieval system, or transmitted in any form or by any means, electronic, mechanical, photocopying, recording, or otherwise, without the written permission of Lindisfarne Books.

All chapters translated by Carla Vlad, except
"The Twelve Worldviews and Anthroposophy,"
which was translated by James Lee;
the introduction was written in English.
Initial editing by Paul V. O'Leary
Cover and text design: William Jens Jensen

Library of Congress Cataloging-in-Publication Data available on request

Print: 978-1-58420-139-7
eBook: 978-1-58420-140-3

CONTENTS

Introduction   vii

1. Goethe and Moses: A Karmic Relationship
   The Free Formation of Judgment   1

2. "Behold, a Virgin Shall Conceive..."
   The Annunciation Scene of Grünewald's *Isenheim Altarpiece*
   Portrayal of an Inspiration   23

3. "The World Is Deep..."
   Friedrich Nietzsche: The Fate of His Spirit and Our Era   29

4. Oscar Wilde and Hubris
   Overcoming Ambition and Vanity
   Wilde's life and his posthumous writing *De Profundis*   39

5. Franz Kafka, Rudolf Steiner, and Norbert Glas
   The Fear of Crossing the Threshold of the Spiritual Realm   63

6. A Friendship under the Guardian Spirit of the Age
   Friedrich Eckstein and Rudolf Steiner   81

7. The Twelve Worldviews and Anthroposophy,
   With a Focus on Anthropomorphism   105

Bibliography   143

INTRODUCTION

The biographical sketches of various representative men offered in this volume were written from the perspective of Spiritual Science. They reveal certain core biographical facts in the complex lives of these individuals and provide a key to some of the riddles found in their strivings and destinies.

Goethe and Moses

In the initial essay on Goethe this key opens perspectives far beyond the horizon of typical "biographical research," including a far-reaching but generally unknown statement by Rudolf Steiner about the karmic link between Goethe and Moses. Precisely one hundred years ago Steiner first alluded to this link in a lecture given in Munich on August 30, 1912. This allusion was triggered by the publication of a scientific essay on Goethe by Konrad Burdach, Professor of German Literature in Halle. The essay, entitled *Faust und Moses,* revealed Goethe's intimate familiarity with Moses's biography, his character and his impulses. Steiner considered Burdach's diligent exoteric research a symptomatic "knocking on the door" of occult truths regarding the fact of reincarnation. Burdach does not explicitly state this, but Steiner did, first in a somewhat veiled way within the lecture mentioned above and later very directly in a private conversation.

It seems noteworthy that Burdach's essay was studied both by Friedrich Eckstein, the influential friend of Steiner's youth, as well as by the well-known Austrian poet Hugo von Hofmannsthal. It is clear that this link provides a key to understanding not only Goethe, but also the deep and, in recent history, tragic connection between the German and the Jewish peoples.

Matthias Grünewald

This short chapter on Grünewald's painting of the Annunciation has been chosen because it contains a riddle that can be solved only in the light of Spiritual Science. The painter, who seems to have had Rosicrucian connections, portrays a sublime moment of inspiration. Inspired cognition is also the principal focus of the essay on Nietzsche.

Friedrich Nietzsche

The sketch on Friedrich Nietzsche outlines his life from the point of view of his extreme sensitivity to suprasensory realities as they reveal themselves, for example, in the interplay between the living and the dead. Nietzsche was a forerunner of the new faculty of inspiration—as Laurence Oliphant was in the English-speaking world.[1] However, since Nietzsche lacked the higher faculty of spiritual-scientific *intuition*, he became a victim of his own inspirations. Intuition is the only mode of cognition free of any sort of deception. That is why inspiration without intuition may mislead the inspired individual—as its essential source is hidden and can only be found by intuition.[2]

---

1. See Laurence Oliphant, *When a Stone Begins to Roll: Notes of an Adventurer, Diplomat & Mystic* (T. H. Meyer, ed.).
2. See the systematic treatment of the difference between *inspiration* and *intuition* in Rudolf Steiner's *Outline of Esoteric Science*.

Rudolf Steiner revealed the suprasensory role that Schopenhauer and Richard Wagner played in Nietzsche's destiny as well as the part he himself was playing in the post-mortem development of Nietzsche after 1900. Material has been used here that was previously unpublished.[3]

Oscar Wilde

The essay on Oscar Wilde focuses on his years in jail, which, viewed superficially, seem to be years of loss, tragedy and failure. In fact, they were his "moment" of disillusion when he acquired insight into the ultimate worthlessness of vanity and personal ambition. From a deeper point of view his years of imprisonment were a period of inner liberation when seeds were planted for a spiritual development that might reach far into the future evolution of Wilde's individuality.

Friedrich Eckstein

Next to Karl Julius Schröer, Friedrich Eckstein was the most influential and inspiring friend of the young Rudolf Steiner. He possessed such universal knowledge in practically all spheres that the Austrian satirist Karl Kraus coined the phrase "whenever the *Brockhaus* [the German equivalent of the *Encyclopedia Britannica*] does not know something, it would descend from the bookshelf and look it up in 'Eckstein.'" He was especially knowledgeable in the history of occultism. In this area he saved Steiner days or months of research. It was he who turned Steiner's attention to Goethe's *Fairy Tale of the Green Snake*

---

3. A more elaborate version of this sketch can be found in my book, *Wegmarken im Leben Rudolf Steiners und in der Entwicklung der Anthroposophie*, Basel, 2012.

and the Beautiful Lily. Only one individual had even more of an impact on the development of the young Rudolf Steiner than Eckstein (and Schröer): his unknown "master," as he confessed in a letter to Eckstein.

Despite his great insight into the world of the occult, Eckstein opposed the necessity of making such knowledge public. For Rudolf Steiner, he was a serious *Retardus* in this respect. Although Steiner later decided to make a great part of occult knowledge available to the general public, it was not done without the most thorough consideration of Eckstein's attitude and conviction in this matter.

※

For the readers of this English edition, a few details may be added that are not contained in the essay of Eckstein drawn from his memoirs *Alte, unnennbare Tage*.

In the 1890s, Eckstein traveled to America and visited Thomas A. Edison in his laboratory in Schenectady, New York, and Mark Twain in Hartford, Connecticut, with whom he forged a close bond of friendship. He was introduced to Harriet Beecher Stowe, the author of *Uncle Tom's Cabin*. When during a period of crisis Twain spent the winter of 1898 in Vienna, Eckstein visited him frequently at his hotel, showed him around the city and guided him to nearby places of interest, such as Heiligenkreutz near Baden, where Crown Prince Rudolph had committed suicide in 1889, the year of Nietzsche's mental breakdown.

Introduction

Rudolf Steiner and the Universality of Anthroposophy

Finally we speak of Steiner himself. To do even minimal justice to his enormous significance for the development of humanity a little essay would be of no avail. Instead, it has been decided to close this little book with a lecture given in Basel in 2008 where I tried to elaborate the essence of four lectures given by Steiner in January 1914, a half year before the outbreak of World War I. Entitled *Human and Cosmic Thought,* those lectures provide a sketch of the twelve fundamental worldviews that are possible to develop. Steiner calls them Idealism, Rationalism, Mathematism, Materialism, Sensualism, and so on (see pp. 109ff). Furthermore, he outlined seven basic cognitive *moods* accompanying them, like Empiricism, Mysticism or Transcendentalism, and so on.

Steiner also considered these lectures a contribution to the peace movement, as they can stimulate mental versatility and develop spiritual tolerance in an age riven by increasing "clashes of civilization."

In these four lectures Steiner makes special reference to Nietzsche. Suffice it to say that Nietzsche is particularly representative of the need to overcome one-sidedness in worldviews and in the corresponding moods.

Whereas most great thinkers like Hegel or Kant represent one or two worldviews or moods in which all their thinking seems to be rooted, in the course of his life Nietzsche underwent a number of radical metamorphoses in his outlook on the world. He was transformed from an Idealist into a Rationalist and ended in the worldview of Dynamism. He also went through various cognitive moods in the course of his development—from "Mysticism" to "Voluntarism." In this sense he was like Goethe, a true forerunner of the universality and mobility of thought, which is one of the key elements provided by Anthroposophy or Spiritual Science.

Spiritual Science itself is like the sun moving through all the twelve worldviews and seven moods. It is as enlightening and impartial as the outward sun, which shines on Materialists, Spiritualists and Sensualists alike.

Representative Men

Each individual portrayed in this book may, beyond his individual uniqueness, be considered representative of one or several aspects of human nature and human striving, and for the obstacles this striving must encounter.

Goethe displays the striving for universal moral, scientific, and artistic values throughout lifetimes, bridging and linking whole ages.

Nietzsche is a, if not *the,* representative of the new faculty of inspiration and of the challenge to complement it by intuition.

Wilde represents the stage of soul development at which insight into the worthlessness of vanity and ambition dawns with the power of a purifying tempest.

Kafka represents those millions of people who are drawn towards the threshold of the spiritual world but lack the courage to cross it.

Eckstein, the great friend of Steiner's youth, is representative of the attitude to withhold occult knowledge from the majority of human beings and keep it as a possession of "the privileged few"—an attitude still prevailing today in certain occult streams.

Introduction

Steiner works to make occult truths public, showing the ways to a radically new knowledge of the spirit and to a new mobility of thought.

In this sense it may be justified to give this little book a title already used by Ralph Waldo Emerson and a subtitle possible only after the birth of Spiritual Science, or Anthroposophy.

My heartfelt thanks go to Paul O'Leary who helped with questions, editing and fruitful criticism and to William Jens Jensen for carefully compiling this book.

Last, but not least: Without the heart and the intelligence put into the translation of these essays by Carla Vlad, this book would not have crossed the ocean.

Michelangelo, Moses, *marble, ca. 1513–15*
(San Pietro in Vincoli, Rome)

GOETHE AND MOSES: A KARMIC RELATIONSHIP

The Free Formation of Judgment

"Pray commend me to Garden Director Lenné some time. I would so much like to traverse with a man like him the field that I, like Moses, can no more than behold from the mountain. From this side of the Jordan and beyond, yours, Goethe."

To Zelter, August 26, 1826

"Germany means nothing, but every individual German means a lot. And yet, they fancy the reverse to be true. Transplanted, scattered all over the world—as are the Jews—that is how the Germans ought to be dispersed in order that the seed of virtue dwelling in them may be matured fully and to the benefit of all nations."[1]

Goethe to Chancellor von Müller
December 14, 1808

1. Preliminary Thoughts

In the spring of 1997 we mentioned in our journal *Der Europäer*[2] the close connection between Johann Wolfgang von Goethe and Jewry, a connection that has been rather neglected

---

1. Translation of the introductory quotes and all other authors cited in this article were prepared by CV.

2. *Der Europäer*, vol. 1, nr. 8, June 1997.

Johann Wolfgang von Goethe, 1828, by Josef Karl Stieler

even by those who take a serious interest in spiritual-scientific matters. The actual implications of this connection were to be elucidated at a later point in time. We present them now below.

The following circumstances have prompted us to render this account. The last years have again and again witnessed some serious accounts of reincarnation experiences relating to the tragic events of the Holocaust. Several of these experiences relate to individual destinies that have passed through incarnations as Jewish people. What we have in mind, above all, are the works published by Rabbi Yonassan Gershom and by Barbro Karlén.[3] These works also cast new light on the question of the connection between the Germanic peoples and Jewry, precisely against the backdrop of the portentous concatenation of events that took place toward the end of the first half of the twentieth century. Yet, little enlightenment will be shed over the aforesaid question unless we consider the connection that Goethe, the polymath, had with both the Germans and the Jews.

2. Konrad Burdach's Revelation

In the *Goethe House* in Weimar the alert eye will not fail to notice that in the "Juno Room" beside the bust of Juno there is also a small bronze copy of Michelangelo's Moses.

Among all the literary specialists who have analyzed Goethe's life the literary historian Konrad Burdach (1859–1936) seems to have been the first to grasp—and not merely by the physical proximity of the statue alone—the poet's underlying affinity with the figure of Moses. To Burdach the issue became

---

3. See Rabbi Yonassan Gershom, *Are Holocaust Victims Returning?*; Barbro Karlén, *And the Wolves Howled*.

the object of a thoroughgoing study. In 1912 he presented the results of his extensive study in a three-part treatise under the title of *Faust und Moses*.[4]

"The figure of Moses," writes Burdach, "is to Goethe, from his youth on, a part of his fervent, never-fading pursuit of a cosmic and intrinsic understanding of the Orient. This kind of understanding was, as always with Goethe, supposed to be founded on one's capacity for empathy and intuition. And these counted with him, virtually from childhood to old age, merely as a means of gaining deeper insight into the nature of the human being. His scientific endeavors, his preoccupation with the Orient and his literary pursuits alike—they all strove to meet their common objective: namely, to fathom the nature of man, his origins, the course of his evolution, the nature of his forces and his purpose. Furthermore, he strove to bring about a full and all-encompassing maturation of his own individuality as the one chosen by the world's spirit to be a guide and mentor able to create and interpret the artistic and genuine truth about humankind."[5]

With scrupulous attention to detail Burdach demonstrates that in Goethe's life, time and again, from his early youth to the end of his life, one may trace a recurrence of the figure of Moses and his five books (the *Pentateuch,* or *Torah*[6]) in the

---

4. Burdach, *Records of the Prussian Academy of Sciences.*

5. Loc. cit., p. 368.

6. The *Torah* is the Jewish name for the first five books of the Bible plus some oral traditions. The *Pentateuch* is the name used by Gentiles and refers only to the five books themselves: Genesis, Exodus, Leviticus, Numbers and Deuteronomy. *Pentateuch* is Greek for "five-volume" book. —ED.

poet's mind. For instance, Goethe's doctoral thesis, which he submitted to the Department of Theology at the University of Strasbourg, was a critical analysis of Moses's Ten Commandments tablets.[7] Furthermore, during the very last conversation between Goethe and Eckermann they happened to talk about Genesis—a detail that, surprisingly, seems to have escaped Burdach's notice.[8]

Goethe's renewed interest in the figure of Moses in 1797 proved to be of the utmost significance; it inspired him to resume his work on *Faust*, which had lain on the shelf for some years. The outer impetus thereto was given by Schiller and their joint work on ballad studies. The outcome of this eager preoccupation with Moses is Goethe's essay *Israel in the Desert*. It provides a unique portrayal of Moses's character, with a thoroughly unconventional approach to the question of the duration of the wandering in the desert—Goethe considers the forty years recorded in the Bible to be far too long. "One can hardly give enough appreciation to the intimate significance that his Moses essay holds for Goethe's inner development as a human being and as an artist," writes Burdach.[9] For this very reason, we shall now quote some excerpts from Goethe's significant, yet little known, piece of writing.

---

7. Burdach, op. cit., p. 390. The dissertation was rejected—presumably on account of its daring thesis.

8. See Johann Peter Eckermann, *Conversations of Goethe with Johann Peter Eckermann*, pp. 421 ff; conversation dated March 11, 1832.

9. Burdach, op. cit., p. 375.

3. Excerpts from Goethe's Essay "Israel in the Desert" (translated by Martin Bidney)

The true, unique, and deepest theme of world and human history, the one to which all others are subordinated, remains the conflict between unbelief and faith. All the epochs when faith rules, in whatever form, are splendid, heartening, and fertile for contemporaries and posterity. But all the eras when unbelief, in whatever form, maintains a miserable victory, even if they temporarily boast an apparent splendor, vanish before posterity. No one wants the torment of admitting what has been fruitless....

I want to draw the reader's attention to two things. The first is the way this strange expedition unfolds from the personality of the commander, who at the start does not appear in the most favorable light. The second factor is my hypothesis that the expedition did not take forty but scarcely two years. This latter consideration will justify and restore to honor the commander whose conduct we earlier had reason to blame. And at the same time it will salvage, and nearly restore in its initial purity, the honor of the national god notwithstanding the inequity of his harshness, which is even more unpleasant than the stubbornness of a people.

So let us first recall the people of Israel in Egypt, in whose great affliction the latest posterity is called on to participate. Among these people, from the violent tribe of Levi, arose a violent man marked by a vigorous sense of what is right and wrong. He appears worthy of his fierce forebears....

He secretly slays the Egyptian who maltreats an Israelite. His patriotic assassination is discovered, and he must flee. There is no reason to ask about the education of one who has committed such an act and presented himself as purely a man of nature. He is supposed to have been favored as a boy by a princess and to have been educated at court, but nothing has had any effect on him. A splendid, strong man, he has remained crude in all circumstances. In his exile, too, we find him a vigorous, curt, taciturn man, unskilled in communication. His daring fist gains him the favor of a princely Midianite priest, who immediately takes him in as one of the family. There he gets to know the desert, where later on he will perform the burdensome duty of a commander-in-chief....

Among such an educated people Moses now lives but, once again, as a separate, reticent shepherd. In the saddest of circumstances for an excellent man not born for thinking and reflecting but keen on action, we see him lonely in the desert, his mind constantly preoccupied with the destiny of his people, always turned to the god of his ancestors. Ill at ease, he feels the effects of exile from a land that, though not the land of his fathers, is still the land of his people. Though too weak to use his fists in promoting this great affair, he cannot devise a plan, and even if he could, he lacks the capacity for any negotiation, any coherent oral performance that might show his personal qualities to advantage. In such circumstances, it would not be at all surprising for such a strong nature to consume itself.

He can derive some comfort through contact with his own people, maintained by caravans going to and fro. After many a doubt he resolves to return and to become the savior of the people. His brother Aaron comes to meet him, and he learns that popular unrest has peaked. Now both brothers can make bold to face the king as representatives....

Already early, even before the expedition reaches Sinai, Jethro comes to meet his son-in-law, bringing daughter and grandson, who had been kept safe in the father's tent during the times of hardship. Jethro proves himself a prudent man. A people like the Midianites, who can move freely wherever they wish and exercise their powers as they will, must be more educated than those who have lived under a foreign yoke in perpetual conflict with themselves and their circumstances. How much more elevated would be the perspective of a leader of these freer people than that of a taciturn, melancholy man, who feels born to act and rule, but to whom nature has denied the means for such a perilous venture.

Moses could not rise to the idea that a ruler need not be present everywhere or do everything himself. On the contrary, by personally intervening he makes his leadership bitter and burdensome. Jethro makes the point clear for the first time and then helps him organize the people and appoint subordinate authorities, something he should have been able to think of on his own....

Unfortunately, Moses had even less talent as a commander than as a ruler....

Several numbers, which may be called round, sacred, symbolic, or poetical, appear in the Bible as well as in other archaic scriptures. The number seven seems dedicated to action, work, and deed. The number forty seems allotted to contemplation and expectation, but particularly to seclusion. The deluge that was intended to separate Noah and his family from the rest of the world swells for forty days. After the waters have remained long enough, they flow away for forty days. For the same period of time Noah keeps the door of the ark bolted. For an equal period Moses stays twice on Mt. Sinai, each time sequestered from the people. The emissaries remain just as long in Canaan, and similarly the whole people, after the same number of wearisome years of being kept apart from other nations, will in the end have confirmed and sanctified an equal space of time. Even to the New Testament the significance of this number is transmitted in its full value: Christ remains forty days in the desert, awaiting the Tempter....

Someone might object: "With great audacity you have denied in an extraordinary man the qualities he has been valued for, those of a governor and of a commander-in-chief. So what made him outstanding? What qualified him for such an important calling? What gives him the temerity to press on in his duties in spite of internal and external disadvantages if he lacks those principal requirements and indispensable talents that you, with unheard of insolence, deny him?" My answer: It is not talents or skills for one thing or another that make the *man of action*. It is the personality that everything depends on. Character is based on personality, not on talents. Talents may be accessory to a person's character; it is not accessory to them. For everything is dispensable to him except himself. So I readily admit that the personality of Moses, from the first assassination through all the subsequent cruelties to his final disappearance, gives a highly remarkable and dignified picture of a man driven by his nature to the greatest deeds. But of course such a picture is thoroughly distorted if we see a strong man of laconic speech and prompt action stumble around for forty years, without either sense or necessity, together with an immense mass of people in such a small area and in direct view of his intended goal. Simply by shortening the way and the time he spends I have mitigated everything derogatory that I had dared to say about him and have raised him to his rightful place.[10]

4. *Moses and Faust*

We have already spoken of the great significance this essay had for Goethe's resumption of his work on *Faust*. Burdach outlines the inner connection between the figures of Moses and Faust as follows.[11]

"We have long observed the motifs of the Moses Legend that Goethe adopts in the final scene of the tragedy, namely Faust's burial by the Lemures, as well as the struggle for the soul of the deceased between the evil spirits summoned by Mephistopheles and the heavenly host descended from above that snatches Faust's immortal soul away from the devils.... However, the analogy between Faust's death and Moses's death does not consist merely in the struggle for the dead body that takes place between the evil and good demons. A *second* parallel is the corresponding motif of the spirits that play a part in the *making of the grave*. The *third* point of similarity lies in the fact that both the hundred-year-old Faust and Moses, who is one hundred twenty years old, defy

---

10. From *West–East Divan: Poems with "Notes and Essays,"* pp. 244—257.

11. Burdach, op. cit., pp. 359 ff.

death. Their resistance will not be broken except by spiritual powers. *Fourth*, there is another parallel in that both Faust and Moses die in their full creative strength, in complete possession of their faculties anticipating the certain fulfillment of the ideal, gazing wistfully at the hoped-for future land that is so near. Yet, the prospect of attaining it themselves will be denied them both. And finally a *fifth* analogy: both Faust and Moses die, leaving a bequest on their deathbed. The last two analogies are the really crucial ones. Herein dwells the soul of the legend of Moses's death. This soul seized Goethe and stirred his poetic imagination into recreating it. Faust—like the founder of the Hebrew nation, the lawgiver who shaped the ethics and faith of the Jewish people, the lawful representative and voice of the Lord, the priestly leader of Israel, dies at the peak of his outstanding life—summoned by God, by God entombed. The Promised Land is within reach, yet he himself cannot enter it. And as he departs this world, he no longer thinks of himself but of future generations to whom he has bequeathed a set of ethical principles.

"However, this Old Testament leader of his people, founder of a religion and prophet, delivered a lot more than this *death*-motif and the noted five outstanding features, as I will show. Likewise Moses's *life,* as the legend envisioned in mystic-poetic terms, inspired Goethe with elements of the Faust drama—not merely the idea for the drama but also for the structure of its plot."

5. *Rudolf Steiner's Reference to Burdach's Work on Goethe*

It will not surprise anyone who has ever sought deeper insight into Goethe's and Rudolf Steiner's works to learn that when depicting karmic relationships that concern Goethe himself, Rudolf Steiner takes into consideration the nature of the poet. One or two words may suffice to reveal a complex feature of Goethe's nature, such as the "open secret." Given the meaning of this phrase and in the spirit of Goethe, it is precisely such profound, karmic and reincarnation-related secrets that cannot and should not be thoughtlessly imparted to the public. They ought not to be exposed to everyone, so to speak. The mode of conveying them should be handled in such a way that the recipient is not simply "served up" a truth; rather, he is called upon to unravel it by his own efforts in a Faustian process of spiritual cognition. Rudolf Steiner's first and, as far as we know, his only reference to Burdach's significant investigations seems to have been approached in this very spirit. Steiner referred to it on August 30, 1912, a few weeks after the third and last part of Burdach's treatise appeared. We quote it below:[12]

"Why is it—and now I'll leave everything else for your soul to divine—that, for all the spiritual elements dwelling in his soul, Herman Grimm failed to cope with the life of Raphael? Do give the answer by means of all that will be needed for the spiritual life of an age that strives to comprehend something like the life of Raphael.... Try to find an answer. You can find it if you let your gaze wander over the first scene that opens our third mystery drama, *The Guardian of the Threshold*. There you find four portraits: Elijah, John the Baptist, Raphael and Novalis.[13] Through what has been brought to

---

12. *Initiation, Eternity & the Passing Moment* (CW 138). "Special lecture" August 30, 1912, is not included in the English edition and remains untranslated into English.

13. The said portraits were used in the mystery drama *The Guardian*

light as a result of years of spiritual-scientific research, which eventually rendered it plausible and solid, we have sought to illustrate how the same soul-individuality reincarnates, goes over from Elijah to John the Baptist, is reborn in Raphael and then reappears in Novalis. Incredible as it may seem today, in not so remote a future it will appear to be just as true that we will fail to grasp the world, unless we turn to the concept of the reincarnation of the human soul and to the karma that traverses several earthly existences. We call it the spiritual interrelationship of the world. Only one who bases his perception on the existence divined by means of Spiritual Science will be able to trace out Raphael's life. In our age the interrelation of spiritual life all over the world enquiringly and insistently confronts the human soul everywhere. It raises questions such as: how do thoughts suddenly emerge in a person's life, as if they sprang from their own soul, thoughts that were there in times gone by and that now re-emerge? One can gain insight into how spiritual life really works, how it causes thoughts to emerge again and again in the course of the ages, provided one is cognizant of the spiritual thought processes that only Spiritual Science can reveal....

"Over the past few weeks something highly significant has appeared in German spiritual life. That I consider it significant may strike you as odd; yet, I am bound to consider it significant, for it is *symptomatically* significant. When I was studying Goethe in Weimar I met many leading personalities in the field of German scholarship. Among the various

---

of the Threshold (scene 1, the ante-chamber to the rooms of the Mystic Brotherhood); in Steiner, *Four Mystery Dramas*.

Germanists I encountered was one who, in my view, showed great promise in his field. I am talking about *Konrad Burdach*, at that time a professor in Halle, who then relinquished his post and became a private scholar. Now over the past few weeks, Konrad Burdach has presented a most interesting treatise to the members of the Academy of Sciences at Berlin. Although, to date, it has only appeared among academic writings, an important question is raised in it. However, it is a question that cannot be answered with Konrad Burdach's methods but only with the methods of Spiritual Science. You realize that anyone musing on the threads of life will naturally come to ask: how is Goethe's Faust linked to the modern soul? Don't we have in Faust the epitome of the practical-minded man of our age, who, having reached the end of his long life, aspires above all to a practical ideal?...

"Bearing in mind that it occurred in the field of philology, what Konrad Burdach has presented strikes us as being of a peculiar nature. When reading his treatise one cannot help thinking: isn't it rather peculiar how pure philology has succeeded in finding a figure from earlier centuries who is analogous to Faust? The old figures return in new guise, as if moulded by Goethe himself. The entire Moses story is set into his time in like manner, as if conceived by Goethe himself. Thereby Konrad Burdach seeks to demonstrate how everything woven around the figure of Moses pours into Goethe's thinking.

"Thus, a person stands on the threshold of the suprasensory world, which answers the following question: To what extent are thoughts and spiritual forces real forces acting throughout time and re-emerging at different ages in accordance with the spirit of

Goethe and Moses: Personal Testimonials

"Still afloat on the surge in my little boat; and as the stars conceal themselves, I am drifting in the hands of Fortune and my bosom is seized with alternating emotions of courage and faith and fear and calm.... I would pray like Moses in the Qur'an: 'Lord, make room in my narrow bosom'..."

Goethe to Herder, soon after July 7, 1772

"By the way, I feel, once again, like the remains of Moses, over which the demons are fighting. Try your utmost and see to it that the venerable father has a decent burial and lies with his forebears in the grove of Mamre."

Goethe to Schubarth, on August 21, 1819

"While looking into the patriarchal vestiges, I ended up in the Old Testament and, once again, I could not wonder enough at the confusion and the contradictions of the Five Books of Moses, which are, as is known, supposed to be compiled from a hundred different oral and written sources. I have made some gracious annotations on the wandering of the Children of Israel through the desert, and a daring thought occurred to me: whether it might be possible that the wide span of time they spent there is a subsequent fabrication? I intend to impart what enkindled this thought in me in a short essay."

Goethe to Schiller, on April 12, 1797

"I went to Schönenhof in the peculiar hope of possibly seeing Goethe there. He came. His brow and his eyes—the image of Moses, full of zeal and spirit."

Father Georg Gessner
on his encounter with Goethe
Zurich, October 22, 1797

※

6. *A Moses Meditation by Rudolf Steiner*

In 1912, a year so significant for a better understanding of Goethe through Burdach, Rudolf Steiner also gave an "esoteric lesson" in which he described a meditation relating to Moses. We render his exact words:

> Many esotericists feel they cannot advance on the paths of esotericism. They think they have mastered their training and they cannot comprehend what obstructs their progress. Since it is difficult to render into present-day words and terms what needs to be said, today there shall be brought before your soul a meditation that all occult students had to undergo in former times.
>
> Just imagine Moses as your teacher and master; imagine the whole matter as a vision. You ask Moses why you cannot go faster in your progress, in spite of your strong yearning to enter the spiritual world. Then you remain silent and await the response, which very often fails to meet your expectations. In most cases the figure of the Golden Calf will appear beside the figure of Moses, then through Moses fire breaks out from the earth and devours the calf. Then Moses dissolves the remaining ashes in water and gives them to the meditants to drink.
>
> It has already been mentioned several times that the human being's powers of recollection are limited to a certain point in the past. What lies beyond that point has

Goethe and Moses: A Karmic Relationship

probably been related to us by our parents, brothers and sisters. We do not recall it ourselves, for our "I" had not yet evolved at that time. Fundamentally, it is the "I" that joins all recollections.

What I mean is the period of your childhood before the process of recollection sets in. Imagine yourself as you were at that time, and now imagine a child in place of the Golden Calf. Then imagine how, through Moses, fire breaks out from the earth, devouring the child, and how we must drink the ashes.

Although in a not so distant past an occult student would have apprehended such a meditation through bare perception, today we need to elaborate on the issue in order to understand it. Some of the things we just said may sound harsh and distressing, but intense and cruel images are necessary to unsettle the soul, if we want to advance in our occult life.

Four thought-impressions ought to be unleashed in our soul by this meditation:

1) The first thought-impression must be to admit that we have really been worshipping the Golden Calf all along. It is our own self, as we have developed it on the physical plane—that is what we have been worshipping. Our recollections are under the influence of Luciferic powers. What we call memory we owe to Lucifer. Lucifer acts in all that we have become through our incarnations and through heredity. If we want the purely spiritual to regain power in us, then our sheaths need to be burned. They need to turn to dust and ashes.

2) The second thought-impression is that what we see and perceive about ourselves from the outside is of no more significance than a bit of dust. But not the kind of dust something new can be produced from and shaped. Rather, it is like a little pile of dust lying on the street—that is how we need to perceive our personality. All sympathies and antipathies must be suspended and held in abeyance. Outwardly we may owe consideration to some

persons, yet inwardly we should be equally disposed toward everyone.

3) We need to awaken the feeling within ourselves that everything surrounding us is nothing but maya. Likewise our bodies, the astral body as well as the etheric, are maya or illusion. What is purely spiritual, what underlies it all, is the "I." Our nose, which has grown along with us, is maya. Our hand is maya. Only when we imagine them as being something that does not concern us in any way—as some ordinary instrument, like a hammer, or something else—only then do we assume the right attitude. Everything surrounding us is maya, is a lie. Moreover, the way we picture ourselves during our youth before individualized memory has set in is a double lie. In the first place, everything is maya; and second, we aren't even able to remember it. Yet, the realization that it is all maya should harden into the certainty that at the heart of it all there is a spiritual force, and that the whole purpose of our being has been incorporated into us by high spiritual entities.

4) Finally, the fourth thought-impression should be that even all the work performed during our earlier incarnations must be annihilated. We need to take our own personality, our own "I," pulverize it and drink it pulverized. This will, though, leave a feeling of desolation, a void in our soul, which will yearn to leave the earthly sphere for serenity, for nirvana. The Buddhist stops at this point, whereas we know that the void must be and can be filled through the Christ-Impulse, by the higher "I," which lifts us back into the higher worlds. This void is always characterized by a feeling of utmost devotion, by the most intimate piety toward the spiritual realms. Care not about your own needs, but think of yourself as God's servant on earth. Think of yourself as a herald from the spiritual worlds.

This is the account of the Golden Calf that, had it not occurred, the Christ-Impulse would not have emerged from the Hebrew people. Call it up before your soul again and again! Not every day, but every three weeks for about a quarter of an hour—and not just two or three times, thinking that will be sufficient. But bring this vision up again and again. Then you'll be certain to realize why you've been unable to make progress.

E. D. N. I.—M. P. S. S. R.

An esotericist who wants to withdraw from his path reveals his own unworthiness. He comes into conflict with the emotions he was seized with when he embarked on the esoteric path. Still, after all is said and done, it would be better if he withdrew from the path than to carry this deception throughout his life.[14]

Some readers may wonder how this "esoteric lesson" relates to the connection between Goethe and Moses, since there is absolutely no mention of the poet in Steiner's notes of March 22, 1912. That certainly is true—however, *the time* when the lesson was given is a Goethe date: March 22 is the date of Goethe's death. Can we really assume that this fact eluded Rudolf Steiner, who had worked so long and intensely in Goethe's spiritual sphere that he was unaware of what day it was when he gave his Moses Meditation?

7. Goethe and Moses

Obviously, neither Steiner's reference to Burdach in August 1912 before members of the Theosophical Society nor his esoteric lesson of March 22, 1912, has prompted any of Rudolf Steiner's students to ask pointed questions about the

---

14. Recorded by Günther Wagner. This esoteric lesson is published in a slightly different version in *Aus den Inhalten der esoterischen Stunden* [*From the Contents of the Esoteric Lessons*], II 1910–1912 (CW 266/2), pp. 349ff.

relationship between Goethe and Moses. That's all the more reason to be grateful for the fact that at least one statement has been passed down when Rudolf Steiner is once said to have directly confirmed their connection in an esoteric lesson, which he elsewhere alluded to as an "open secret." Thanks to Father Rudolf Meyer (1896–1985)—who also wrote a noteworthy book on Goethe (*Goethe: The Heathen and the Christian*[15]—this statement has been recorded. When asked about it,[16] Meyer gave the following answer on April 19, 1984: "It wasn't me whom Rudolf Steiner addressed with this statement. I heard from Mr. Schröder, the then branch head in Bremen—where I gave a lecture on Goethe—that in an esoteric lesson given approximately in 1920 Dr. Steiner spoke of Goethe's having been Moses in his Egyptian incarnation. Yet, I've not heard this from anyone else since. That is why I am hesitant to talk about it."

8. Closing Remarks

Even if the above statements can only be used "hesitantly" and with caution, they may shed a completely new light on Goethe's comments on both the Germans and the Jews. This seems to us to be of the utmost importance for the future development of these two peoples and for the relationship between them. For, just as the Jewish people once worshipped the Golden Calf and needed Moses to prevent them from further partaking

---

15. *Goethe, der Heide und der Christ.*
16. The question came from Dr. H. von Volkmann, Freiburg i. Br., to whom the author feels indebted for the kind permission to quote Rudolf Meyer's answer. Branch head Schröder is, presumably, Johannes Gottfried William Schröder (1870–1942).

in idolatry, so a serious reconsideration of the true spirit of Goethe might well help the Germans in future to fully vanquish the Golden Calf of Nationalism and of Mammonism—which they succumbed to in the twentieth century—instead of bringing ruin upon themselves and others.

We leave it to our readers to assimilate the few statements compiled here and to elaborate upon them further.

"BEHOLD, A VIRGIN SHALL CONCEIVE..."

The Annunciation Scene
of Grünewald's *Isenheim Altarpiece:*
Portrayal of an Inspiration

Grünewald's *Isenheim Altarpiece* in Colmar, France, is one of the great works of Western art. As always with great art, its substance is not exhausted at first glance. Upon steady and careful contemplation, some of the "secret revelation" of this piece of art will gradually unveil itself to the eye of the beholder.

Let us now examine the altarpiece[1] (one part of the multi-panel work): here the painter obviously depicts the Annunciation scene from the Gospel of Luke. Yet into it he weaves certain elements and processes that are not found in the Gospel account, thus indicating that he does not aim at rendering a traditional, historical-naturalistic representation. We shall examine some of these elements and facts.

The prophet Isaiah looks down onto the situation in the sacral chamber below.

Mary is immersed in reading a chapter of Isaiah (7:14).

The left hand page of the opened book reads as follows: *"Ecce virgo concipiet et pariet filium et vocabitur nomen eius Emmanuel. Butyrium et mel comedet ut sciat reprobare malum et..."* Translated this reads, "Behold, a virgin shall conceive

---
1. See ill. 1.

and bear a son, and shall call his name Immanuel.... Butter and honey shall he eat, when he knoweth to refuse the evil, and..."[2] At the top of the right hand page, two words conclude the verse: *"eligere bonum,"* or "choose the good."

After that, a space is left, followed by the first verse of the left hand page, which is repeated literally: "Behold, a virgin shall conceive, and bear a son, and shall call his name Immanuel." Thus, *both* pages are inscribed with the very same words.

Did the painter choose to repeat precisely this verse merely for the purpose of filling the right hand page, which would otherwise have been left empty, as is suggested in an art guide? And yet, for that purpose he could just as well have painted a further or another passage from Isaiah. On closer examination this duplicate cannot be explained by considering its outer aspect only—for Grünewald has, in truth, painted an inner process. He actually shows Mary reading the prophetic verse from Isaiah *twice*. First, she reads it as a devout Jewish woman immersed in the Scriptures of her people. She reads the verse as an objective element in the stream of religious prophecies, just as any other member of the Jewish community would have read it. But she is reading it in the presence of the Holy Spirit, gently symbolized by the dove hovering in the midst of the process, and in the presence of Gabriel, who—with his garments still streaming behind him—has just wafted through a spiritual portal and into the sacral chamber.

Under the inspirational influences of the Holy Spirit and Gabriel, Mary beholds the verse for *the second time*, now with

---

2. Translation from *The American Standard Version of the Holy Bible*: http://www.ebible.org/bible/asv/.

"Behold, a Virgin Shall Conceive…"

Detail of the angel and Bible

Believed to be a portrait of Matthias Grünewald

a newly inspired spiritual awareness. Solemnly called upon by Gabriel, with a note of urgency in his mien and by the motion of his hand and finger, she now may assume that the verse concerns her own being.

Thus, Matthias Grünewald portrays the way Mary's contemplative, selfless immersion in the prophecy of Isaiah turns into an act of inspiration that makes her grasp the full meaning the prophecy holds *to her*. Therefore, the very same verse appears twice: once perceived objectively, and once perceived through an inspired awareness by her who reads it as relating to her own being.

That is the "open secret" of the duplicate text in the book that lies open before her.

Now we can grasp the reason for the spiritual presence of the prophet in the room. Since he remains closely linked with his prophecy, he maintains a presence in the sacral room even at the moment the prophecy comes true in a spiritually real way. However, unlike Gabriel and the dove, he is not actively involved but merely beholding the process of fulfilment from the spiritual world and finding the *truth* of his prophecy *sealed* at that very moment.

Thus, on closer examination, we realize that this panel is a metaphorical-symbolic portrayal of a moment of *inspiration*, to wit: one of the most subtle and sublime, one of the most significant and profound inspirations ever experienced.

Through the symbolic representation of this historic moment of inspiration, Matthias Grünewald has proved himself to be highly cognizant of spiritual facts and processes.

Whoever beholds this painting more than *once* can learn the key to the faculty of perceiving *these* very processes and facts.

Friedrich Nietzsche, *1906*
Oil on canvas by Edvard Munch

"THE WORLD IS DEEP..."
FRIEDRICH NIETZSCHE: THE FATE OF HIS SPIRIT AND OUR ERA

SILS-MARIA

Here I sat, waiting—not for anything—
Beyond Good and Evil, fancying
Now light, now shadows, all a game,
All lake, all noon, all time without all aim.
Then, suddenly, friend, one turned into two—
And Zarathustra walked into my view.[1]

Nietzsche and Sils-Maria[2]

Is there any mountain scenery more sublime, which frees your spirit better than the scenery surrounding Sils-Maria and Lake Sils?[3] Friedrich Nietzsche, who was highly sensitive to both spiritual and physical climates, enjoyed regular summer sojourns at this place during his last period of active creativity, from 1881 until his breakdown in Turin in January 1889. While he was walking along the shore of Lake Silvaplana[4] in August 1881, a great thought suddenly descended upon him—the vision of the eternal recurrence of all events—"6,000 feet beyond humanity and time." It was a great thought indeed, for he was steering toward the idea of reincarnation, although slightly caricatured. It was there that Zarathustra came to life or, as Nietzsche himself put it:

---

1. Nietzsche, *The Gay Science,* trans. by W. Kaufmann.
2. Sils-Maria is a small mountain village located in southeastern Switzerland SW of St. Moritz.
3. Lake Sils adjoins the village of Sils-Maria.
4. Lake Silvaplana is a short distance northeast of Lake Sils.

Sils and Lake Sils (above); Nietzsche's summer house in Sils

"The World Is Deep..."

> "Then, suddenly, friend, one turned into two—
> And Zarathustra walked into my view."

Nietzsche went there many summers, again and again "all lake, all noon, all time without all aim." It was there that he raised himself aloft to the idea of the *Übermensch,* the "Overman,"[5] that appeared to him embodied in Zarathustra—the epitome of the higher evolution of all human beings. Nietzsche's Zarathustra is the great hymn of praise to the higher development of the human spirit.

A visitor to Surlej[6] and Lake Sils is reminded of these great moments in Nietzsche's later works by the memorial stone at the Silvaplana Lake and by the Nietzsche plaque at the Chasté peninsula,[7] which is inscribed with a quote from *Thus Spoke Zarathustra*:

> O Man! Attend!
> What does deep midnight's voice contend?
> "I slept my sleep,
> And now awake at dreaming's end:
> The world is deep,
> Deeper than day can comprehend.
> Deep is its woe,
> Joy—deeper than heart's agony:
> Woe says: Fade! Go!
> But all joy wants eternity,
> Wants deep, deep, deep eternity!"[8]

---

5. Here the translator (CV) follows Walter Kaufmann's translation of Nietzsche's *Übermensch*. See Kaufmann, *Nietzsche: Philosopher, Psychologist, Antichrist*. In chap. 11, Kaufmann explains why he opts for rendering the term into English as "overman" (in contrast to "superman" etc.).

6. Surlej is a small village located near St. Moritz and Silvaplana.

7. A finger of upland jutting into Lake Sils.

8. Nietzsche, *Thus Spoke Zarathustra* (trans. by R. J. Hollingdale).

Nietzsche described the Chasté peninsula to his sister in these words: "Our peninsula has no equal that I'm aware of, neither in Switzerland nor in any other part of Europe."

At the close of this prodigious period of creativity with its flights of imagination, the spiritual turn in Nietzsche's fate was beginning to loom on the horizon. Alongside his other writings the increasingly polemical and eventually fully spirit-denying works emerged: *The Case of Wagner*, *The Antichrist* and *Ecce Homo*. His decline into madness overcame him in January 1889 and lasted for eleven years.

Rudolf Steiner and Nietzsche

A visitor to the Nietzsche house[9] in Sils will encounter a notable eyewitness: Rudolf Steiner.

On January 22, 1896, Nietzsche's sister took Steiner to the patient's room in Naumburg[10] where her brother lay wrapped in mental darkness. The written account of this visit is one of the most impressive documents of the Nietzsche house in Naumburg. Steiner was granted a glimpse into the original, as yet unprinted, manuscripts of *The Antichrist* and of *Ecce Homo*. He once called Nietzsche "the greatest mind of our time."[11]

We may truly say, without the slightest exaggeration, that Rudolf Steiner loved no other contemporary writer as much as he loved Nietzsche, in the most profound, emphatic sense. Once when he filled out answers to a jocular questionnaire, Steiner answered the question: "Who would you like to be,

---

9. The Nietzsche house in Sils is now a museum (see page 30).

10. Naumburg, a small city (population 20,000 circa 1895) located about 25 miles northeast of Weimar.

11. In a letter to Anna Eunike from Naumburg, Jan. 1896 (CW 39).

if not yourself?" as follows: "Friedrich Nietzsche—before he went mad." For Steiner, Nietzsche would have been, as it were, the ideal reader of his *Philosophy of Freedom*. Nietzsche would have found in it what he was yearning for: new impulses of cognition and ethics springing from the strength of an autonomous, free personality.

Steiner admired the boldness of Nietzsche's philosophy, his free and unfettered power of thought. Steiner's deep empathy with the tragic fate that befell Nietzsche in 1889 sprang from this source. Steiner's book *Friedrich Nietzsche: Fighter for Freedom*, originally published in April 1895, bears witness to his capacity to identify himself with the latter, to be able to shed a higher light onto Nietzsche's significant thoughts, and even more, onto the *sources* of his thought.

The Heights and Hazards of Inspiration

It is, then, hardly surprising that Steiner sought to pursue a thorough, spiritual-scientific investigation of Nietzsche's fate, which had such a deep affect upon him, especially since he also regarded Nietzsche as the embodiment of a very significant impulse of his age. Inspired by Nietzsche's soul, it was borne in upon Steiner that humankind, having dwelled for thousands of years in spiritual darkness, was beginning to aspire again toward the spiritual realm, striving for concrete *inspiration* that springs from the spiritual. Yet, he was also aware of the perils hovering over humankind lest the faculty of inspiration should not be enhanced through *intuition*, which is rooted in man's capacity to rise above sensory experience to pure thinking. In other words, Steiner was aware of the danger of receiving inspirations without knowing, or without even wanting to know *from where they come*, from which spiritual beings they originate. Thus, in the course of his life, Nietzsche was strongly inspired by different spirits, above all by the so-called dead who came to him, for instance: from the history of Greece; during his early period by the late Schopenhauer; and, in his later period, by a spiritual being to whom the historical Zarathustra had already pointed—Ahriman. Above all *The Antichrist* and *Ecce Homo* (the latter was not published until 1909) should be seen within the context of the last-mentioned source of inspiration. Nietzsche was the *medium* for these writings rather than their author. According to Steiner's spiritual research, these works were written by Ahriman himself. In these writings "Ahriman has already begun to appear as an author, and his work will continue."[12] Beginning with Theodor Herzl's *Judenstaat* (The Jewish State) to Hitler's *Mein Kampf* (My Struggle), and up to that most influential propagandist, Samuel Huntington, writing *The Clash of Civilizations*—all these works are inspired more or less by Ahriman. Likewise, we encounter the phenomenon in the artistic field. Among countless other examples, we can often observe the influence of ahrimanic sources of inspiration in the staging of Richard Wagner's works. This, in fact, is not too difficult to perceive.[13]

Richard Wagner's "Good Deed"

If this chain of events had not been interrupted, Nietzsche's thought process would have become largely ahrimanic. Yet, he was shielded to some extent by virtue of an influence from

---

12. July 20, 1924; *Karmic Relationships,* vol. 6 (CW 240).

13. See the article by Gerald Brei; see also the bibliography.

the realm of the dead. Steiner's spiritual research has revealed the source of this beneficent influence. It is the individuality of Richard Wagner who, after his death in 1883, observes the unfortunate turn of events in the life of his former friend, in whom he found a kindred spirit and who, according to Steiner, "bestows upon him the benefaction of having him fall into mental darkness at the right moment; he shields his consciousness from entering perilous regions."[14]

Madness—a "good deed"? Whoever wants to grasp the meaning of this insight must learn to reshape his mode of thinking. It calls for a "revaluation of all values" inherent in the criteria previously applied to such matters. From an "earthly" perspective, a mental breakdown is, of course, a tragedy. From a spiritual perspective, however, in the case of Nietzsche it proves to have prevented something even worse from happening.

Whereas in his anti-Wagner work, Nietzsche spiritually "eviscerates" his once venerated friend Wagner, this generous friend, from beyond the threshold of the spiritual world, "bestows upon him the act of benefaction of having him fall into mental darkness." Anyone who is unaware of Wagner's great humanity may gain an idea of it now.

Rudolf Steiner's "Good Deed"

Two seven-year-cycles after Friedrich Nietzsche's death on August 25, 1900, Steiner made a significant, new communication about Nietzsche's postmortem development in a private lesson given in Basel on June 1, 1914, Whit Monday. The records of the lesson are not contained in the collected edition of Rudolf

---

14. Nov. 11, 1917 (CW 178).

Steiner's works.[15] The above-mentioned passage, quoted here for the first time, reads as follows:

> A personality of the nineteenth century, who was not capable of grasping the spiritual as long as he was in his physical body, has passed away. In this post-mortem existence in the spiritual world he stands exposed to the danger of losing his intellect to Ahriman. I have been struggling with Ahriman for years in order to return his own intellect to this human being.

Rudolf Steiner does not say Nietzsche's name, but what other individual could he be discussing?

It is obvious that, despite Wagner's protective "good deed," his "act of benefaction," Nietzsche's soul would have—*in its subconscious*—fallen prey after death to Ahriman. Although Nietzsche was unaware of it, the ahrimanic influence had a deep impact on his soul before he collapsed into madness. His last writings offer eloquent testimony to this fact. Thus, after Nietzsche's death, Steiner, through a spiritual battle, carried forward the seemingly paradoxical spiritual act of love initiated by Wagner. In this manner he has smoothed the way for the development of Nietzsche's individuality, a development more favourable than the one he would have had without *this* additional "good deed."

Nietzsche's Fate as a Question to Humankind

Rudolf Steiner introduced his far-reaching comments on his struggle for a favorable post-mortem development for Nietzsche:

> We find ourselves within human evolution; we live inside it. Our era is a particularly important and significant one.

---

15. The record of this esoteric lesson is kept in the archives of Perseus Publishing, Basel, Switzerland.

"The World Is Deep..."

> One human faculty has reached a stage that is particularly important in our time: the faculty of thinking. And, what is of crucial importance for this evolution is the way in which man will make use of this faculty."

Nietzsche's life was brought to a halt at the threshold when a new spiritual light had dawned on humanity after the Kali Yuga had come to a close in 1899. It is called Spiritual Science, or Anthroposophy. His spiritual destiny presents a monumental question to the people of his and also of *our own time:* do you want to reshape your thinking so that it will learn to grasp not only the facts of nature but also *spiritual facts* by means of the faculty of thinking, which was denied to me in spite of my deepest yearning for it? Or do you want to fall prey, like me, to the powers of Ahriman, to the anti-Zarathustra, who is the embodiment of the *Untermensch,* the "underman"? The answer to this question can be provided only by each person, individually, with each answer coming about in its own, individual way.

Friedrich Nietzsche's spiritual fate carries within itself a torch of freedom glowing for the whole of humanity. That is why his destiny has such profound, contemporary relevance. "Deeper than day can comprehend."

For a deeper understanding of the "Nietzsche riddle," the reader may want to turn to what Rudolf Steiner's spiritual research has to say about the most recent incarnation of Nietzsche. See *Karmic Relationships,* vol. 1, the lecture of March 15, 1924.

Oscar Wilde, 1889

OSCAR WILDE AND HUBRIS

OVERCOMING AMBITION AND VANITY
WILDE'S LIFE AND HIS POSTHUMOUS
WRITING, *DE PROFUNDIS*

The following contributions were made during the Oscar Wilde Conference, organized by Marcus Schneider for May 31 to June 1, 2008, at the Scala Basel, where the eurythmy ensemble Eurythmiegruppe Stuttgart (directed by Elisabeth Brinkmann) performed Wilde's one-act play Salomé. *The play premiered in 1896 while its author was serving his sentence in Reading Gaol. The presentation has been edited and some passages expanded.*

Dear Ladies and Gentlemen!

Yesterday we witnessed an impressive performance of Oscar Wilde's significant play, *Salomé*. The play can provide a key to understanding Wilde's whole life, in that his life also epitomizes a process of spiritual growth. Whoever looks at the surface of Oscar Wilde's biography is likely to miss the spiritual aspect. A superficial glance at Wilde's life might tempt us to pronounce a precipitate judgement: a prodigious rise followed by a terrible fall into perversion, sinfulness and failure. It depends upon one's point of view. Such an attitude allows for no more than a maya point of view. For, in truth, Wilde's last years are marked by a profound psychological change. To prove this we need to cast a brief glance at his life.

I. The Glorious Ascent

Oscar Wilde is born in Dublin on October 16, 1854. His father pursues various interests; he is a doctor, an eye and ear specialist. He also writes books on archaeology and one on Jonathan Swift. Wilde's mother is a writer who translated works of literature and takes pride in her Florentine origins. Oscar has an elder brother, William Wills, and a younger sister, Isola Francesca, who dies at the age of ten.

Wilde attends Trinity College, enthuses over classical languages and the ancient world, particularly over Greece. He shows no inclination toward the natural sciences. Rather, he develops into a thoroughgoing aesthete and delights in occasionally displaying the snobbish traits of a dandy. With his classics tutor and friend, Reverend Mahaffy, he travels to Northern Italy and visits Milan, Venice and Padua.

Upon leaving Trinity College Wilde goes to Oxford and studies art history, history and aesthetics and graduates with a Bachelor of Arts. He encounters well-known personalities of his day who have a great influence upon him. Among them was Walter Pater who championed the *l'art pour l'art* concept. Another is the more prominent John Ruskin, one of the Englishmen who, as an art historian, discovered the importance of Italy. For several years Ruskin lived in Venice—the guest house *La Calzina* on the Zattere bears a stone plaque preserving the memory of his sojourn—and almost literally eyed up every single stone of the Venetian edifices. The result is his monumental work *The Stones of Venice*. A tinge of this love of the South and of Renaissance art flashed over to Wilde. Moreover, it was Ruskin who paved the way for the aestheticist Empire-theory. Cecil Rhodes was one of his students and disciples.

Thus, in an atmosphere of great erudition, of refined aestheticism and the self-evident belief in England's imperial mission the young Wilde comes of age. He travels to Greece and Rome and makes his literary debut with a poem entitled "Ravenna," for which he is awarded a prize. Ravenna—the city where Dante died; to him Wilde would come to feel a growing spiritual kinship.

In 1879, the Michael Year, Wilde moves to London where he lives for the next two seven-year cycles. He goes on a lecture tour to America. He writes essays. Everything runs like clockwork; there seem to be no obstacles to his artistic career. In 1884 Wilde marries Constance Lloyd, who bears him two sons. Wilde works for the *Pall Mall Gazette* and edits the journal *Woman's World*. In 1888 he publishes a collection of fairy tales; in 1890 his famous novel *Dorian Gray* comes out.

In 1891, around the time of his second lunar node, the portentous encounter with Lord Alfred Douglas occurs—a young man aged twenty-one, the man who seemingly turns out to have ruined Oscar Wilde. Lord Douglas was of aristocratic descent, yet belonged to a kind of decadent aristocracy founded on pride and prestige rather than on genuine values. The intellectual levels of the two friends were highly discrepant, and what Alfred loved most about Oscar was the latter's fame and popularity. He loved Wilde "on the pedestal" and was hoping to work his way up on Wilde's achieved glory. Wilde fell in love with the young man with blond hair and fair skin. His novel *Dorian Gray* had just been published. The protagonist's forename alludes to an association with homoeroticism. As every connoisseur of Ancient Greece knows, the practice of homosexuality was ascribed to the *Dorians* who had settled in pre-classical Greece. Wilde gave Alfred an autographed edition of *Dorian Gray* and helped the not quite excellent student with an exam at Magdalen College in Oxford. It evidently is a fateful encounter, whose story and context may well reach back into previous earth lives. Conventional psychological terms are inadequate to explain the unfathomable drama that unfolded between and around these two people in the years to follow.

In December 1891, the very year he met Lord Alfred Douglas, Wilde writes the play *Salomé* in French in Paris. Perhaps it is precisely these peculiar circumstances and turn of events that throw light on the intricately aestheticized nature of the play, whose dialogues reach distinct mantric cadences at intervals.

In 1893 the original French version is published, after British censors had initially refused publication of an English version. Only in the following year is the English version licensed to come out. Its translation into English is provided by Lord Douglas.

For the poet the translation came to be a source of dissatisfaction and pain, since it was teeming with "schoolboy faults," as Wilde put it. Even so, Wilde tolerated with indulgence and generosity his friend's inadequate literary competence.

Then the last of Wilde's plays is created, *The Importance of Being Earnest*, perhaps his most brilliant and wittiest social comedy. It is a cutting satire on the shallowness of British aristocratic mores and a fireworks display of fierce sarcasm, in part masterly disguised as pleasurable delicacies. Thus writes a man "on the pedestal" who believes he has the world at his feet and that it gratefully, or at least respectfully, welcomes whatever he sprinkles among the wide public.

II. The Descent

The staging of the play, which is a great success, is immediately followed by the prelude of the next chapter in the playwright's life. In the club Wilde frequents in Alfred's company, Alfred's father, Lord Queensberry, leaves a visiting card with an insulting message: "To Oscar Wilde posing as a somdomite"—a misspelled term denoting a homosexual, and in a broader sense, a term for any sort of "perverted" sexual behavior. Two factors favour this course of events: Queensberry's evident eagerness to become a talking point in public as well as a law previously amended in England for stricter control of homosexual practices (the Amendment Act). These laws, meant to safeguard Victorian societal pretence, are obviously applied selectively only to those who dared to assume a non-hypocritical attitude and who overtly foster their inclinations.

Queensberry wants to make the public think that he is striving to rescue his son from a profligate. However, Bosie—as Wilde soon came to call his friend—abused Oscar financially, ran up debts at Wilde's expense, always wanting to dine in the finest clubs and restaurants. Only the most expensive wines could please him, with everything put on Wilde's bill. Moreover, he rang Wilde's doorbell intuitively at the very moments when the latter was going to work. For Bosie's sake Wilde would often postpone his work for hours, only to find that Bosie would selfishly claim the saved hours for himself.

How does Oscar Wilde respond to Queensberry's denigratory attack? At this stage Wilde is firmly convinced that he can lord it over the public and need not tolerate anything of this sort. At first he believes he can give the "funny little" aristocrat a bop on the nose with the help of a solicitor and institutes a libel suit. But all of a sudden everything goes awry and things take a different turn. In the course of the trial letters are made public, letters that the father received from his son, which the latter received from Wilde. You know well what can be read into a letter, if minded to do so. Male prostitutes are called to the witness box. A father–son tragedy is also dragged into the scandal. Issues are over-hyped.

The whole affair becomes public knowledge, and the masses increasingly derive pleasure from the case. A storm is brewing. Who is going to win? Oscar Wilde, the world-famous writer, or the powerful British society that Wilde had often enough exposed to mockery? Wilde's solicitor, as well as his close friends, advise him to leave the country and wait for the dust to settle on the matter. Had he followed their advice, Wilde would undoubtedly have escaped conviction. Yet, he would have considered the alternative to be an act of cowardice. He didn't want to evade the challenge—not *that* way. He wanted to chance a test of strength. To him, pride and vanity were not compatible with flight. These two motivating forces of Wilde's remarkable character make him underestimate the true societal balance of power. Out of the blue, the Queensberries from all over Great Britain creep out of their hiding places and, strengthened by herd instinct, seek revenge on the writer.

In May 1895, Wilde is imprisoned and sentenced to two years' hard labour, the maximum sentence allowed in a case like his. He is convicted of "gross indecency" committed in private with same-sex persons. Wilde has become, so to speak, the first exhibit confirming the authority of the Amendment Act.

III. *The Return of the Prodigal Son*

We have now come to the genesis of this man's *spiritual* turning point and shall dwell upon this aspect in detail. My attention was drawn to this spiritual layer in Wilde's life by virtue of a survey written by Daniel N. Dunlop.[1] In 1905, Dunlop reviewed the first abridged edition of Wilde's notes taken in prison, which had just been published under the title *De Profundis*. It was the most stirring book he had ever read, as Dunlop himself asserted. Dunlop directed his attention to the psycho-spiritual, almost alchemical, metamorphosis that Wilde's soul had undergone in prison, a process that *De Profundis*—written in the form of a long letter to his friend Bosie—bears unique witness to. Dunlop's review, translated into German, was printed in the May 2008 issue of *Der Europäer*. Wilde's psychological development is usually underestimated or simply ignored. Yet it seems to me that it contains within it the very seeds of his entire *subsequent* development that will extend into succeeding earth lives. One must not be misled by the fact that in the three years *after* his release Wilde did not produce any significant writings and that he occasionally fell into his former faults and foibles. Thus, he meets Bosie again, and even while in exile in Paris he fosters relations with a whole lot of, more or less, beautiful young men. He visits Rome once again; Pope Leo XIII receives him in seven

---

1. See "Cited Works." Dunlop was an occultist, Theosophist, and later an Anthroposophist and friend of Rudolf Steiner. See T. H. Meyer's biography, *D. N. Dunlop: A Man of Our Time*.

private audiences. In Paris he has an operation performed on his ear—possibly indicating a certain spiritual hearing loss—and dies on November 30, 1900, at age 46 in the *Hôtel d'Alsace*, Quartier Latin, after having received a conditional baptism and the last rites. Today, the house bears a memorial inscription commemorating his stay there.

From the point of view of his spiritual growth the final phase of Wilde's life is rather insignificant when compared to the time spent in prison. A psychological-spiritual change as experienced by Wilde need not, and probably cannot, manifest itself in the same life. But a new soul resides and stirs within the old body.

At this point, let us cast a fresh glance through other people's eyes at some of the attributes Wilde possessed when entering this phase, so as to better understand their profound metamorphosis.

One of Wilde's contemporaries, a playwright himself, observes: "In a certain sense Mr. Wilde is to me our only thorough playwright. He plays with everything: with wit, with philosophy, with drama, with actors and audience, with the whole theatre." The quotation, from George Bernhard Shaw, sees in Wilde a man who plays with everything.

Another poet writes:

> My first meeting with Oscar Wilde was an astonishment. I never before heard a man talking with perfect sentences, as if he had written them all over night with labour, and yet all spontaneous.... I noticed, too, that the impression of artificiality that I think all Wilde's listeners have recorded came from the perfect rounding of the sentences and from the deliberation that made it possible.... I think, too, that because of all that half-civilized blood in his veins, he could not endure the sedentary toil of creative art and so remained a man of action, exaggerating for the sake of immediate

effect every trick learned from his masters, turning their easel painting into painted scenes.

Wilde's contemporary witness—William Butler Yeats—emphasizes the playwright's tremendous ease and mastery in creating language and artistic form. Brilliance and elegance of style flowed from his pen.

And finally one more instance:

> An aesthete! That isn't saying much. Walter Pater [one of Wilde's tutors at Oxford] was an aesthete, a man who revelled in the enjoyment and re-creation of beauty, and life he revered with coyness and demureness, replete with decency. An aesthete is by nature thoroughly decent. Yet Oscar Wilde was utterly indecent, replete with tragic indecency. His aestheticism was something like a tense pain. The precious stones that he was pretending to explore with elation were like shattered eyes numbed with the inability to bear the sight of life. He was ceaselessly sensing the impending doom of life. He was perpetually shrouded in tragic anxiety. He was relentlessly tempting providence. He was insulting the world of appearances. And he was sensing how fate was lurking in the dark only to pounce on him from the shades.[2]

It was Hugo von Hofmannsthal who wrote this portrayal of Wilde. However, I do not share his view of Wilde's having continuously scented a sense of fatality that hung over him. He was a genuinely reckless epicure who savored his imprudence to the full until misfortune befell him.

Overnight, he is goaded out of all his bonds and commitments, out of all the public prestige. Fame had been his constant companion for many years. Wilde was a pivotal literary

---

2. Funke, *Oscar Wilde*, p. 168 (trans. CV).

figure for numerous young poets; he embodied a new aestheticism in literature, overflowing with inspiration and creativity. He even wrote fairy tales. At the same time he vies with fate and displays a sort of graceful vanity, rather than a shallow one devoid of grace. At times he deliberately acts like a snob. He believes he is made for exceptions, not for rules, as he himself claims. And now he loses everything: prestige and position, wife and children—in other words, all those values modern society deems worth striving for.

As a tribute to his genius Constance offers him an allowance, yet on condition that he should never see Bosie again. She dies in April 1898 without the married couple having ever met again.

We shall now turn our attention to the experiences Wilde undergoes in prison where, after early 1896, he begins writing a letter of denunciation, justification and vindication to his friend Bosie. It is, in fact, a love letter, even if not in the traditional sense of the word. Wilde considers it his duty not only to unsparingly account for his own deeds and misdeeds, but also to open his young friend's eyes to the latter's own flaws. He feels jointly responsible for Bosie's turning a blind eye to certain foibles, as he himself has encouraged them by his own indulgence and tolerance.

Soon after his conviction Wilde is faced with incidents that begin to trigger a chain of sweeping changes within him.

Now I shall read some passages from *De Profundis*.[3] I begin with a crucial experience in Wilde's life that clearly exemplifies

---

3. The manuscript was written on prison paper between January and March 1896. Before that, Wilde was not granted permission to write. Every page filled was taken away from him. In the end

the contrast between his social position before and after the decisive event.

> On November 13, 1895, I was brought down here [to Reading Gaol] from London. From two o'clock till half-past two on that day I had to stand on the centre platform of Clapham Junction in convict dress and handcuffed, for the world to look at. I had been taken out of the Hospital Ward without a moment's notice being given to me. Of all possible objects I was the most grotesque. When people saw me they laughed. Each train as it came up swelled the audience. Nothing could exceed their amusement. That was of course before they knew who I was. As soon as they had been informed, they laughed still more. For half an hour I stood there in the grey November rain surrounded by a jeering mob.
>
> For a year after that was done to me I wept every day at the same hour and for the same space of time. That is not such a tragic thing as possibly it sounds to you. To those who are in prison, tears are a part of every day's experience. A day in prison on which one does not weep is a day on which one's heart is hard, not a day on which one's heart is happy.
>
> Well, now I am really beginning to feel more regret for the people who laughed than for myself. Of course, when they saw me I was not on my pedestal [an expression Bosie used to illustrate how he preferred Wilde]; I was in the pillory. But it is a very unimaginative nature that only cares for people on their pedestals. A pedestal may be a very unreal thing. A pillory is a terrific reality. They should have known also how to interpret sorrow better. I have said that behind Sorrow there is always Sorrow. It were still wiser to say that behind sorrow there is always a soul. And to mock at a soul in pain is a dreadful thing. (*De Profundis*, p. 937)

---

he was allowed to read and correct everything in context.

In order that he can endure prison life Wilde says to himself: "*At all costs I must keep Love in my heart.*" He realizes that nobody can be ruined except by his own hand. He awakens to a sense of responsibility toward each and every thing that unfolds. He gains that level of merciless self-knowledge that anyone who nurtures spiritual aspirations is sooner or later certain to experience.

At one point he writes from prison:

> My friends must face the fact that...I am not in prison as an innocent man. On the contrary, my record of perversities of passion and distorted romances would fill many scarlet volumes...and so, though the particular offence required by the law did not find a part amongst my perversities of passion, still perversities there were, or else why am I here? It may be a terrible shock to my friends to think that I had abnormal passions, and perverse desires, but if they read history they will find I am not the first artist so doomed, any more than I shall be the last. (*The Complete Letters of Oscar Wilde*, pp. 784–787)

As we can see, there is a remarkable harshness in his self-analysis. What's more, Wilde explicitly demands that one of his friends listen to what has really occurred, as a chance for their friendship to survive. He wants his friends to know this facet of his life as well, and then either go on accepting him, or turn their back on him.

In prison Oscar Wilde also experiences sublime and deeply stirring episodes, which to others may seem to be but trifling matters to be ignored; yet, they leave a lasting impression on him—acts of kindness that bear the seeds of a strong impetus to inner metamorphosis. The following is a beautiful example. It concerns one of Wilde's friends who stood by him through thick and thin: Robert Ross, referred to as Robbie.

> Where there is Sorrow there is holy ground. Some day you will realise what that means. You will know nothing of life till you do.... When I was brought down from my prison to the Court of Bankruptcy between two policemen, Robbie waited in the long dreary corridor, that before the whole crowd, whom an action so sweet and simple hushed into silence, he might gravely raise his hat to me, as handcuffed and with bowed head I passed him by. Men have gone to heaven for smaller things than that. It was in this spirit, and with this mode of love that the saints knelt down to wash the feet of the poor, or stooped to kiss the leper on the cheek. I have never said one single word to him about what he did. I do not know to the present moment whether he is aware that I was even conscious of his action. It is not a thing for which one can render formal thanks in formal words. I store it in the treasury-house of my heart. I keep it there as a secret debt that I am glad to think I can never possibly repay. It is embalmed and kept sweet by the myrrh and cassia of many tears. When Wisdom has been profitless to me, and Philosophy barren, and the proverbs and phrases of those who have sought to give me consolation as dust and ashes in my mouth, the memory of that little lowly silent act of Love has unsealed for me all the wells of pity, made the desert blossom like a rose, and brought me out of the bitterness of lonely exile into harmony with the wounded, broken and great heart of the world. (*De Profundis*, p. 906)

There are other numerous, arcane and genuine exegeses on Sorrow and its potential to be transmuted into new ethics and beauty. The spirit of the artist pervades the lines.

Wilde reads through the Old and New Testaments, and he studies *De imitatione Christi* by Thomas à Kempis. He takes a close look at the life of St. Francis of Assisi. When he speaks of Christ, he does so above all to elucidate the question: why is Christ of such tremendous significance to the *arts* in the time to come?

A few further examples illustrate Wilde's spiritual immersion that was setting in:

> Most people live *for* love and admiration. But it is *by* love and admiration that we should live. If any love is shown us we should recognise that we are quite unworthy of it. Nobody is worthy to be loved. The fact that God loves man shows that in the divine order of ideal things it is written that eternal love is to be given to what is eternally unworthy. Or, if that phrase seems to you a bitter one to hear, let us say that everyone is worthy of love, except he who thinks that he is. Love is a sacrament that should be taken kneeling, and *Domine, non sum dignus* should be on the lips and in the hearts of those who receive it. I wish you would sometimes think of that. You need it so much. (*De Profundis*, pp. 930–931)

Another passage allows us to gain insight into this alchemical soul-furnace where fundamental properties of the soul are transformed or moulded into being. Once again Wilde speaks of Christ: "In a manner not yet understood of the world he regarded sin and suffering as being in themselves beautiful, holy things, and modes of perfection. It *sounds* a very dangerous idea. It is so. All great ideas *are* dangerous. That it was Christ's creed admits of no doubt. That it is the true creed I don't doubt myself.

"Of course the sinner must repent. But why? Simply because otherwise he would be unable to realize what he had done. The moment of repentance is the moment of initiation. More than that. It is the means by which one alters one's past" (*De Profundis*, p. 933).

Here is one more relevant excerpt:

> Christ, had he been asked, would have said—I feel quite certain about it—that the moment the prodigal son fell on his knees and wept he really made his having wasted his substance with harlots, and then kept swine and hungered for the husks they ate, beautiful and holy incidents in his life. It is difficult for most people to grasp the idea. I dare say one has to go to prison to understand it. If so, it may be worthwhile going to prison. (*De Profundis*, p. 933)

And, finally, a passage indicating the inner change taking place in Wilde:

> St Francis of Assisi...God had given him at his birth the soul of a poet, as he himself when quite young had in mystical marriage taken Poverty as his bride; and with the soul of a poet and the body of a beggar he found the way to perfection not difficult. He understood Christ, and so he became like him. We do not require the *Liber Conformitatum*[4] to teach us that the life of St. Francis was the true *Imitatio Christi*: a poem compared to which the book that bears that name is merely prose. Indeed, that is the charm about Christ.... He is just like a work of art himself. He does not really teach one anything, but by being brought into his presence one becomes something. And everybody is predestined to his presence. Once at least in a person's life each one walks with Christ to Emmaus. (*De Profundis*, pp. 933–934)

---

4. A collection of texts (compiled by Fra Bartolomeo in the fourteenth century) comparing the life of St. Francis of Assisi with Christ's life.

IV. Stages of Christian Initiation

The passages cited, which could easily be expanded, elucidate the way a person comes to tread the path of Christian initiation—without originally having striven for it, that is, without having sought it in a deliberate or conscious pursuit over the years. From a higher spiritual standpoint one could speak of it in terms of a prenatal resolution made by that self that, in the context of hierarchical beings, predetermines the manner of its re-birth. The first stages of Christian initiation are clearly perceivable in the sequence of events in Wilde's life beginning with the year 1895: detention, flagellation and the Crowning with Thorns—we need only think of the experience at Clapham Junction. The implication of foot washing can also be inferred. Through suffering, Wilde has realized that it is more important to serve others than one's own petty self, as impressive as this self may seem to the world. As to the remaining stages of the Passion and to the extent their completion was brought about in the case of Wilde—this is left to the reader to decide.

Wilde undergoes all these phases when *Salomé* is premiered. It is staged on February 11, 1896, the very time when Wilde is writing *De Profundis*. In this context the two writings are related to each other. In *De Profundis* Wilde portrays his own *psychological* Baptist-like destiny. He, too, is beheaded, for he indeed loses everything that had hitherto been essential to him: glory, prestige, literary independence, his friends and his family.

As Marcus Schneider mentioned yesterday in his reflections, it was probably not pure chance that these twists of fate in Oscar Wilde's life were unfolding shortly before the Kali Yuga came to an end—i.e., at a pivotal moment in history when a new spiritual light was beginning to pour into humankind. With his soul having tread a burdensome and agonizing path, Wilde emerges as a seeker after that very light. Therefore, he may be regarded as an archetype of the many spirit-seekers who become clairvoyant by experiencing a Passion of the soul.

V. From Lucifer to Christ

In a figure analogous to Wilde's fate we can identify a kind of archetypal key in the history of humankind. At the same time it can, in a way, symbolize an example both as a pattern to be followed and an admonishment to recoil from, to whomever goes in spiritual quest now and in the future. For the time being let us turn to the archetype. We encounter him in the crucial moment of transition when Jesus of Nazareth, after having laid aside the "I" that had clothed his personality, sets out for the banks of the Jordan and for the Baptist, where the Christ "I" is to enter the selfless sheaths of Jesus. On his way, this "unique being" (as Rudolf Steiner calls the Jesus-sheaths freed of the "I") has three encounters: with two Essenes, with a leper and then with a man who seems to have been through an ordeal similar to Oscar Wilde's.

> The wretched man [upon encountering the portentous sheaths-being] felt the urge to thus speak to this being. "In my life have I attained high ranks. And at all times as I rose to new ranks, I felt at ease, and many a time was I overwhelmed with a thought, saying to myself: what an exceptional man you must be if your fellow men raise you to such heights, if you have achieved such great success upon earth. What an outstanding man you are! I was blissfully happy. Yet it happened that I soon lost this bliss. It happened in *one* night. And once, as I had just fallen

asleep, a dream came over me with such intensity that I dreamt I was feeling ashamed of dreaming such things. I dreamt a being was standing in front of me asking: who then, has raised you to such greatness? And who has led you to so high a rank? I felt ashamed, wondering how it was conceivable at all that such a question be put to me in my dream. For it was plain to me that I was exceptional, and that I had obviously attained the high ranks by means of *my* great virtues. And as the being had spoken to me thus, I was filled in my dream with an ever deeper growing sense of shame toward myself, in my dream"—thus did the wretched man speak to himself. "Then I took to flight, but no sooner had I fled than the vision appeared anew in another shape and said: '*I* have raised you and taken you to a high rank.' And in him I perceived the Tempter of whom the Scriptures tell that he had been the Tempter in the Garden of Eden before. Hereupon I awoke, and I have found no peace of mind ever since. I gave up my rank, deserted my home, my everything, and henceforth have I been wandering about, idling away the time. And now my path leads me to you, a stray man, a beggar." And the very moment the man had uttered the words (the akashic record has it), the wraith reappeared and positioned himself before Jesus of Nazareth, who in the same moment disappeared. Whereupon the vision vanished, and the man was abandoned to his fate. (trans by CV)

These are Rudolf Steiner's words in a lecture on the Fifth Gospel presented on December 10, 1913, in Munich. He talks about an archetypal occurrence. Pride goes before a fall, the proverb says. A man is portrayed, a man full of self-conceit, a man to whom the spirit of hubris that has guided him is *revealed* in his fall. It is Lucifer. The revelation is profound.

This awareness dawns on Oscar Wilde in a similar manner; the artist's soul has attained initiation through the experience of sorrow. Yet, with him it does not occur in an encounter with the sheaths-being but in the encounter with the real Christ with whom "once at least in his life each man walks...to Emmaus," as Wilde writes in *De Profundis*.

So we are faced with a kind of archetype of human evolution—inasmuch as luciferic forces have a hand in it. The challenge for man is to unravel it.

There is a further relevant aspect in Wilde's experience: the descent into the depths of our own soul where selfhood is confronted. It represents one of the two fundamental trials of the soul that the modern spirit-seeker is predestined to experience. In the lecture cycle *Wonders of the World, Ordeals of the Soul, Revelations of the Spirit* Rudolf Steiner shows that it pertains to the painstaking quest of the modern spiritual seeker to reach the two extreme poles of soul ordeals. Striving toward the outer world, he is seized by a terrible sense of void. He gets lost if he is not capable of taking Christ with him. At the opposite pole he enters his own self. What does he find there? Ferocious egoism. He can get burned on it if he's not capable of taking Christ along, or in Rudolf Steiner's own words:

> The Christ impulse has the quality of working as a disintegrating force, as a destructive influence upon our selfishness, our egoism. How peculiar; the deeper we descend with the Christ impulse into our own selves, the less able egoism is to harm us. We then enter deeper and deeper into our own inner selves, and by penetrating with the Christ impulse through our egoistic drives and passions we learn to perceive the human being. We come to know all the secrets of this wonder of the world, which is the human being. Indeed, the Christ impulse enables us to go much further. If we were deprived of it [while

descending into our inner self—TM], we would bounce back like a rubber ball and would be unable to enter our own selves, down into the sphere of our own inner constitution. But with Christ, we permeate through ourselves, and we emerge out of ourselves, so to say, on the opposite side. So that if we go out into the universe finding the Christ principle everywhere in the widths of space, we also find on the other side—if we penetrate below into the nether world—all the impersonal, freed from our own selves. Either way, we find something that transcends our selves. In the universal spheres we are neither dissolved nor atomized, we find the world of the upper gods; below we enter the world of the true gods.[5]

As we can see, while in prison Oscar Wilde realized much of what is required on this second path.

VI. *Epilogue*

After having witnessed here on these two days a beautiful presentation that throws a new light on Oscar Wilde's life and work within the framework of the anthroposophic movement and the Anthroposophical Society, we can now ask: How can Wilde's life acquire meaning for people in a spiritual-scientific movement? In what way does it inspire emulation or caution? Wilde's life can reveal how the lower self can free itself from vanity, for instance. The process of purification from vanity in Wilde's case is a radical one. Every person with spiritual aspirations will undergo it in the long run.

According to a remark made by Rudolf Steiner to Walter Johannes Stein, there are three enemies of the soul that are harmful to life: Ambition, Vanity and Untruthfulness. But in a

---

5. Lecture, Aug. 27, 1911 (trans. by CV).

spiritual movement, he added, they have a *devastating* impact.[6] I think the time will come when the rather tragic events in the history of the Theosophical, and later Anthroposophical, Movement and Society in the course of the nineteenth and twentieth centuries will be reconsidered *under the aspect of this very statement made by Steiner.* For it gives a clue as to the primary motives behind the conflicts and tragic developments of those organizations. It will be more fruitful than thousands of pages of justifications and vindications, or of denunciations and apologias. Steiner's word is emblematic of the crux of all these grave, rather fatal, developments.

We see in Oscar Wilde a man who is thoroughly prepared for his next incarnation upon earth to be wary of falling prey for a second time to the three aforementioned vices, especially the vice of vanity—vices very difficult to perceive since they are situated in a realm where one can get burned unless one enters it with the guidance of Christ. It also takes courage to realize that these vices must be completely eradicated for the very reason that they have not only a harmful, but also an absolutely *devastating* effect upon spiritual development.

If regarded from this point of view, Oscar Wilde's life functions as a compelling example of the need to overcome these three terribly plain and yet so challenging traits—ambition, vanity and untruthfulness. Therein lies the premonitory nature of his life.

On the other hand, it also shows that it is possible—in his case through a profound soul-ordeal rooted in the fatal implications of an erstwhile karmic involvement—for the lower self

---

6. See *Mitteilungen aus der anthroposophischen Arbeit in Deutschland*, no. 38, Michaeli 1966.

to decrease, so that the higher "I" in us—the Christ "I"—can increase, to use the words of the Baptist. Through this process the soul assumes the shape of a chalice that receives something higher than itself. The soul, thus, becomes the Holy Grail. This is the development Oscar Wilde strove for in his greatest and most majestic moments and eventually brought to completion. And *this* is what posterity will remember him for—rather than what some biographers have deemed to be of major importance and what they have meticulously recorded—namely, the incidents and occurrences he experienced after his release from prison, which occasionally let him relapse into former frailties.[7]

Whoever unsparingly pursues his own quest for self-knowledge and hereby undergoes a purgatory process as Wilde did, or experiences a similar purification from vanity, will realize the uselessness of such a quality of the soul. The eminent Laurence Oliphant equally toiled his way through to this awareness, though with him it was a process of deliberate self-education. He who unsparingly directs the acquired cognitive faculties at his own self—as we know, it is easier to apply merciless scrutiny to *others* than to oneself—can, even in the worst turmoil of the soul, cry out with Oscar Wilde not "What an ending! What an appalling ending!" but "What a beginning! What a wonderful beginning!"

---

7. Wilde's sole literary production on his release from prison was *The Ballad of Reading Gaol*—which here cannot be dealt with in further detail—portraying the fate of a fellow prisoner sentenced to death and hanged.

Franz Kafka, in his late twenties

FRANZ KAFKA, RUDOLF STEINER, AND NORBERT GLAS

The Fear of Crossing the Threshold of the Spiritual Realm

As Franz Kafka was still hoping to recover from his grave lung and laryngeal tuberculosis in Dr. Hoffmann's sanatorium in Kierling near Vienna in the spring of 1924, another doctor joined the group of doctors already attending him: the twenty-seven-year-old Norbert Glas (1897–1986), who had just opened a practice in Vienna. The patient and his young girlfriend Dora Diamant (1898–1952) wanted to try their *utmost,* so they decided to consult an *anthroposophical* doctor as well; at least Dora Diamant must have been aware of his background. In his very last letter, written to his parents on the day before his death, Kafka describes Glas as a man "who greatly inspires me with confidence."[1] But not even Norbert Glas could avert his approaching death. Franz Kafka died on June 3, 1924, at noon.

The fact that Norbert Glas appeared at Franz Kafka's sickbed prompts us to reflect upon Kafka's relationship to Anthroposophy and to Rudolf Steiner.

---

1. Franz Kafka, *Briefe an Ottla und die Familie;* excerpt trans. by CV; letter dated June 2, 1924.

It was probably in Berta Fanta's salon in Prague that Kafka heard of Rudolf Steiner (1861–1925) for the first time[2]; his friends Max Brod (1884–1968) and Felix Weltsch (1884–1964) may also have inspired him to pursue the study of Anthroposophy. In the spring of 1910, Kafka had attended spiritualist séances with Brod. Brod found Steiner's foundational guide *How to Know Higher Worlds and Its Attainment* "very inspiring," even though he could not decide upon pursuing extensive studies of Anthroposophy.[3]

What we know for certain is that Kafka possessed three writings of Steiner in his library: *The Education of the Child in the Light of Anthroposophy*, the writing *Haeckel, the Riddle of the Universe and Theosophy* as well as *Our Atlantean Ancestors*, published in 1909 (later on incorporated into the book *From the Akasha Chronicle*).[4]

We also know that, in March 1911, Kafka attended Rudolf Steiner's lecture cycle *An Occult Physiology* (CW 128) in Prague. Steiner delivered the lectures from March 20 to March 28. Together with Brod, Kafka also attended Steiner's public lectures on March 19 and 25. Berta Fanta's daughter Else observed Kafka during Steiner's lectures. She wrote: "I remember having observed that during the lectures Franz Kafka's eyes were sparkling with pleasure and a smile irradiated his face with joy."[5]

---

2. See H. Binder, *Kafkas Welt—Eine Lebensgeschichte in Bildern*, p. 200. In the following we will quote from this thorough and excellently documented chronicle published in May 2008.

3. G. Gimpel, *Weil der Boden selbst hier brennt, Aus dem Prager Salon der Berta Fanta (1865–1918)*.

4. Binder, op. cit., p. 200.

5. Ibid, p. 201; excerpt trans. by CV.

The Encounter with Rudolf Steiner

When the lecture cycle was over, Steiner offered personal consultations on March 29 and 30. Franz Kafka was among those who also sought counsel. He went to see Steiner in the Hotel Victoria on March 29.

Kafka records the visit in his diaries. He describes to Rudolf Steiner his dilemma of not being able to reconcile the necessity of earning money in his insurance job, which he calls his "bread-and-butter job," with his literary pursuits. He wants to know from Steiner whether studies in Theosophy might further aggravate the already existing dilemma. He writes: "Now these two professions [the bread-and-butter job and writing] could never tolerate each other and accept a shared fortune. The least good fortune in one is a great misfortune in the other. If I have written something good one evening, the next day in the office I am on fire and can't get anything finished. This back-and-forth is getting steadily worse.

"In the office I fulfil my duties outwardly, but not my inner duties, and each unsatisfied inner duty turns into an unhappiness that never stirs out of me. And to these two endeavors, never to be balanced, shall I now add Theosophy as a third? Will it not disturb them on both sides and itself be interrupted from both? Will I, presently such an unhappy person, be able to carry these three to a conclusion? I have come, Herr Doctor, to ask you this, for I feel that if you consider me capable of it, I, too, can really take it upon myself.

"He listened very attentively, without seeming to attend to me in the least, entirely devoted to my words. He nodded from time to time, which for him seemed to be an aid to strict concentration."[6]

Kafka was twenty-eight years old when this conversation took place. That is the time when a person's spiritual guidance by his angel withdraws. It is the moment when a person needs to pass into a state of complete independence. However, even at this critical moment in his life, Kafka still needed guidance in order to make this momentous decision. The impetus to decide in favor or against Theosophy he now expects to come *from someone else*.

From Kafka's concluding sentence, which only focuses on Steiner's head cold, we can gather that Rudolf Steiner did not assume responsibility for the former's decision. Indeed, as an initiate of spiritual development based on *freedom* he was not even *allowed* to do so.

---

6. Franz Kafka, *Tagebücher 1909–1912*, pp. 29f; the excerpts quoted here are from the translation by Paul Kerschen in *The Diaries of Franz Kafka 1910–1923*, see: http://kafka.metameat.net/archives/191103.php?en. Two days after their conversation, Kafka sent Steiner a sample of his work—at the latter's request. There is no information as to what Kafka sent and no record of Kafka's reply. Kafka's covering note (there is a facsimile in *Beiträge zur Rudolf Steiner Gesamtausgabe*, no. 109, Michaeli 1992, p. 48) is dated March 31, 1910, which Binder considers to be a misdate.—Several years later (1952), Max Brod, to whom Kafka spoke about the conversation, wrote the minutes from memory, in which he creates the impression that Steiner misunderstood Kafka (*Der andere Rudolf Steiner*, pp. 191ff.). It is possible that Kafka perceived it that way, in retrospect. The crucial *freedom-element* in the above-mentioned conversation seems to have eluded both Kafka and Brod. Steiner certainly would not have liked Kafka to pursue the study of Theosophy, as it were, simply out of a sense of "duty" or under an influence from without. The question was whether he really wished to do it, out of his *own* free *will*.

Had he—against his principles grounded in freedom—encouraged Franz Kafka to pursue all "three," then the latter would have probably followed Steiner's advice at first, as he obviously had great confidence in Steiner at that moment. Later on though, beset by renascent doubts concerning the dilemma between his occupational and literary pursuits, he would perhaps have blamed Theosophy and Rudolf Steiner, rejecting both.

It was essential that he make the decision out of his own free will. It had to be a decision arising from his "I." Kafka could not bring himself to do so. Thus, he tarried, as it were, at the portal leading to the realm of suprasensory cognition, where he had been compellingly drawn by his deeper soul and spirit forces—not the least because of his previous experiences at Steiner's lectures.

※

My visit to Dr. Steiner

A woman is already waiting (up on the third floor of the Victoria Hotel at Jungmannsstrasse) but insists that I go in before her. We wait. The secretary comes with promises. Down the corridor, I catch a glimpse of him. Immediately afterward, he comes up to us with half-extended arms. The woman explains that I was the first to come. I walk behind him now as he directs me into his room. His Kaiser gown, which on lecture evenings seems mopped black (not mopped, but rather radiant in its own blackness) is now by daylight (at three in the afternoon) dusty and even spotted, especially on the back and shoulders. In his room, I try to show my humility, which I cannot feel, by looking for

REPRESENTATIVE MEN

Rudolf Steiner and Franz Kafka, 1910

a ridiculous place for my hat; I put it on a small wooden rack for lacing boots. In the center, a table, I sit with a view of the window, he on the left side of the table. Some papers on the table, with a few drawings recalling one of the lectures on occult physiology. A small volume of annals in natural philosophy tops a short pile of books; other books lie around elsewhere.

You cannot look around now, for he keeps seeking to hold you with his gaze, and if he fails at it once, you must look out for the gaze's return. He begins with a few loose sentences: So you are Dr. Kafka? Have you been interested in Theosophy for long? But I press forward with my prepared speech: I feel as if a large part of my being is drawn to Theosophy, but at the same time I have the greatest fear of it. I am afraid of it bringing new confusion, which would be terrible for me, seeing as my present unhappiness consists of nothing but confusion. The nature of the confusion is this: my happiness, my abilities, and any possibility of using them have always lain in literature. And here I have even experienced states (not many) that, in my opinion, lie very close to the clairvoyant states you describe, Herr Doctor, in which I lived entirely within each idea, but also fulfilled each idea, and in which I felt myself not only at my own bounds, but also at the bounds of all humanity. Only the ecstatic peace that may be unique to the clairvoyant was missing from these states, though not quite entirely. I leave out of this that I have not written my best work in these states. Currently I cannot devote myself entirely to these literary pursuits, as I should, and for various reasons. Apart from my family situation, I could not live from literature alone because of the slow development of my work and its particular character. In addition, my health and my character prevent me from devoting myself to a life that is uncertain at best. So I have become an office worker at a social insurance institute. Now these two professions could never tolerate one another and accept a shared fortune. The least good fortune in one is a great misfortune in the other. If I have written something good one evening, the next day in the office I am on fire and cannot get anything finished. This back-and-forth is getting steadily worse.

In the office I fulfill my duties outwardly, but not my inner duties, and each unsatisfied inner duty turns into an unhappiness that never stirs out of me. And to these two endeavors, never to be balanced, shall I now add Theosophy as a third? Will it not disturb them on both sides and itself be interrupted from both? Will I, presently such an unhappy person, be able to carry these three to a conclusion? I have come, Herr Doctor, to ask you this, for I feel that if you consider me capable of it I, too, can really take it upon myself.

He listened very attentively, without seeming to attend to me in the least, entirely devoted to my words. He nodded from time to time, which for him seemed to be an aid to strict concentration. At the beginning a silent cold disturbed him; it ran out of his nose; he kept working at it with his handkerchief deep in his nose, a finger on either nostril.[7]

※

To decide out of his own free will to integrate Theosophy into his life of turmoil would certainly have taken a lot of courage. At first the forces of fear held sway over the forces of courage.

Before the Law

Kafka's subsequent writings can be regarded against the background of his inability to cross the threshold of the spiritual world. The short story *Before the Law*,[8] written in the late autumn of 1914, provides a prime example of this phenomenon. It was incorporated into the penultimate chapter of the novel *The Trial*, published only posthumously, although the story was published several times on its own during Kafka's lifetime, first in 1915.

The story describes the dilemma of a "man from the country" who wishes to gain entry into the law; yet, the gatekeeper

---

7. Ibid.
8. The following quotations from Kafka's story *Vor dem Gesetz* are taken from the translation by Ian Johnston, see: http://records.viu.ca/~johnstoi/kafka/beforethelaw.htm.

denies his request, putting him off until later. However, the man does not turn away from the law and its stern guardian after all, but settles on its threshold, spending his whole life there, neither outside of it "in the country," nor inside "in the law." The man leaves no stone unturned to win over the gatekeeper, who subjects him again and again to brief interrogations. Yet the man fails in his attempts to persuade him. He grows old, unlike the gatekeeper who does not seem to age. His eyesight grows weak. As he nears the end of his life, "he recognizes...in the darkness an illumination that breaks inextinguishably out of the gateway to the law." Standing now on the threshold of death, he rouses himself to put one last question to the gatekeeper: "Everyone strives after the law...so how is it that in these many years no one except me has requested entry?" The distressing reply that concludes the story reads as follows: "Here, no one else can gain entry, since this entrance was assigned only to you. I'm going now to close it."

In his short story, Franz Kafka has captured something of the Michael Age, which began in 1879. According to Rudolf Steiner, the whole of humankind has thenceforth been treading unconsciously on the threshold of the spiritual realm ("the law").[9] After the period of materialism, which has lasted for centuries, humanity is again receptive to and in need of spiritual experiences. Every individual now passes unconsciously into the realm of the spiritual world. Yet, if he does not want to come into conflict with the experiences he undergoes unconsciously, he needs must become *conscious* of this fact that is to be

---

9. For example, on Sept. 12, 1919 (CW 193).

explored through Spiritual Science and must try to harmonize his inner and outer development with this very fact.

Thus, he may gradually step across the threshold consciously, thereby bringing to fruition the deeper evolutionary tendencies of his own being.

Such is the challenge that awaits every individual today—namely, the task of becoming aware of his own unconscious spiritual strivings. It is, so to speak, the *primordial spiritual task* of modern man. The inability to cope with it, on the other hand, may be described as the *primordial spiritual conflict* of the modern individual.

Rudolf Steiner showed a methodical path leading across the threshold "into the law" that also nurtures moral evolution. On this path the occult student has to become familiar with the harsh demands of the guardian of the threshold, who must reject anything that falls into discord with the world of the "law." At the end of the seventh so-called lesson, the guardian speaks to the student thus: "You may enter. The gate is open. You will become a true human being."[10]

Whereas Rudolf Steiner acted, as it were, as an example to humanity by crossing the threshold of the spiritual realm in a sensible, courageous and thoroughly conscious manner, Franz Kafka embodied the very fear of stepping across the threshold, a fear that hinders human consciousness from crossing the threshold and that dominates so many people.

---

10. In Kafka's story the gatekeeper represents both the lesser and the greater guardian. He is, so to speak, a blend-caricature of the two guardians. Cf. the way they are depicted in *How to Know Higher Worlds and Its Attainment* (GA 10); excerpt trans. by CV.

"I'm Caught in an Iron-hard Web"

Kafka's inability to decide upon crossing the threshold of the spiritual world—the first step of which still is a thorough, systematic study of Spiritual Science—determined the attitude he later had toward Steiner. It increasingly assumed an ambivalent, indefinite and vague character.

This became quite obvious in a conversation held around 1921 with his much younger friend Gustav Janouch (1903–1968). Janouch wanted to hear Kafka's opinion about Steiner and asked: "Is he a prophet or a charlatan?"[11] Since Kafka's reply is revealing of his spiritual indecision as well as of his attempts at dwelling therein, we offer the rest of their conversation:

> "I don't know," declared Kafka. "I'm not clear in my mind about him. He is an uncommonly eloquent man. But this is a talent that also belongs to the armory of the trickster. I'm not saying that Steiner is a trickster. But he could be. Deceivers always try to solve difficult problems on the cheap. The problem Steiner is concerned with is the most difficult one there is. It is the dark division between consciousness and being, the tension between the circumscribed drop of water and the infinite sea. I believe that in this matter Goethe's view is the right one. One must, with quiet respect for the unknowable, accept the order of everything that is knowable. The smallest thing, like the greatest, must be close and precious to one."
>
> "Is that also Steiner's view?"

---

11. G. Janouch, *Conversations with Kafka*, trans. by Goronwy Rees. Hartmut Binder questioned the reliability of Janouch's records. However, Kafka's statements on Steiner seem plausible enough to us, especially since they refer to a direct question of Janouch.

Kafka shrugged his shoulders and said: "I don't know. But perhaps that's my fault, not his. Steiner is alien to me. I cannot get close to him. I am too involved in myself."

"You're a chrysalis!" I said, laughing.

"Yes," Kafka said seriously, "I'm caught in an iron-hard web without the slightest hope that one day a butterfly may fly out of my cocoon. But that, too, is only my own fault—or to put it better—it's the ever-recurrent sin of despair."

"And your writings?"

"They're only attempts, scraps of paper thrown to the winds."

We had reached the corner opposite the general post office.

Kafka extended his hand.—"Forgive me. I have an appointment with Brod"—and with long strides hurried across the road.

"That Kafka Was at Least Nurturing Fresh Hopes..."

Based on the above we shall finally take a close look at the part Norbert Glas played at the end of Kafka's life. For this purpose we shall quote a personal note from Glas to Kafka's biographer, Hartmut Binder, first published in 2008.

On May 21, 1974, fifty years after the event, Glas wrote to Binder:

> It must have been in the spring of 1924—in April, if my memory serves me right—when a lady called me from Vienna to Kierling near Klosterneuburg to see Kafka and to give him medical advice. I still remember, it was a rainy afternoon as I reached the place. It must have been a Saturday or a Sunday. It was a plain building; I think they called it a "sanatorium." A young lady, Dora Diamant, welcomed me and took me to a very emaciated patient lying in bed. Kafka's face was ashen, with hollow cheeks and fever glistening in his eyes. His voice was

Franz Kafka, Rudolf Steiner, and Norbert Glas

Dora Diamant, 1928

Norbert Glas, 1926

Franz Kafka, 1923

rather quiet and hoarse. One could see at once that he was suffering from a most severe tuberculosis. The diagnosis made by Prof. Hajek was also presented to me. Both Kafka and Miss Diamant sought me to recommend some method of treatment, yet I can hardly remember what I suggested. It was one of the phosphorus tablets, probably a special iron salt made up of pyrites. Naturally, I prescribed a restorative diet and medications for external use, but I cannot recall.

Miss Diamant must have known of my ties with Rudolf Steiner and Anthroposophy, since that was the real reason for which I had been called.

The conversation in the hospital room was very cordial and I had the impression that Kafka was at least nurturing fresh hopes.[12]

According to Kafka's last letter to his parents, written with the help of Dora Diamant on the day before he died, Glas "would visit [him] three times per week, modestly going by tram and by bus." The subjects they touched upon during the conversations are nowhere recorded.

However, we learn something else that sheds new light on the last weeks of Kafka's life. Hartmut Binder writes about an unpublished letter that Robert Klopstock wrote to Kafka's parents. Klopstock (1899–1972) was a young doctor who had been friends with Kafka and who, together with Dora Diamant, attended to Kafka up to the hour of his death. According to Klopstock, "Glas made a very good impression on Kafka, who trusted him. However, he *was somewhat sad* (even though he accepted it) to hear that Glas was an anthroposophist."[13]

---

12. Binder, op. cit., p. 675; excerpt trans. by CV.

13. Ibid., p. 675; italics by THM; excerpt trans. by CV.

It is obvious that, irrespective of his medical attendance at Kafka's sickbed, Norbert Glas evoked recollections—perhaps even associated with stirring experiences—of his encounter with Steiner and his relation to Anthroposophy, irrespective of whether and what they had talked about Anthroposophy. Kafka's sadness at finding that Glas was an anthroposophist betokened his regrets about having spiritually dwelt in the "sin of despair" in spite of the encounter with Steiner and his illuminating Anthroposophy. He was sad at having tarried "*before* the law" instead of courageously crossing its threshold.

Franz Kafka suffered all kinds of torments, fears and turmoils that may arise out of such *tarrying* on the threshold (*Before the Law*). Thus, he has become a representative figure and a projection for millions of people and for their fear of stepping across the threshold of the spiritual realm. He has become the very living embodiment of this fear. The conflict between his two "professions" as well as his dread of social ties were spiritually rooted in his tarrying on the threshold. Perhaps they could have been solved by a courageous penetration "into the law."

We have only to consider seriously the concept of a postmortem evolution and of future earthly lives to value the impact of Norbert Glas's appearance at Kafka's sickbed for the subsequent development of Franz Kafka's spirit-soul. The "young doctor who greatly inspires me with confidence" brought a kind of spiritual glimmer of hope to the man who was doomed to die, some of that "illumination that breaks inextinguishably out of the gateway to the law." *This* "medication" will—even though it tastes bitter at first—have an impact much more profound on the further development of Kafka's individuality than the phosphorus tablets.[14]

※

The author would like to refer the reader to the valuable work of Peter Selg, who rendered the life and work of Rainer Maria Rilke and Franz Kafka from the anthroposophic medical perspective: *Rainer Maria Rilke und Franz Kafka—Lebensweg und Krankheitsschicksal im 20. Jahrhundert*, Dornach, 2007. See also a noteworthy essay by Maja Rehbein: *Alles ist in den besten Anfängen—Der Arzt Norbert Glas und der Dichter Franz Kafka*, Novalis, no. 5/6, 2002.

---

14. For a symptomatic analysis it may be important to know that when Norbert Glas met Kafka, he was the same age as Kafka when he met Steiner.

Friedrich Eckstein

A FRIENDSHIP UNDER
THE GUARDIAN SPIRIT OF THE AGE

Friedrich Eckstein and Rudolf Steiner

"There have been two occurrences in my life that I hold to have been of such far-reaching import to my life and my being that, I dare say, I would have become quite another person, had these events not emerged as they have. About one of them I will remain silent; yet the other I must voice: it is the circumstance of my having encountered *you*. *What* you *mean* to me surely you know better than I do; what I know is that I owe you an immeasurable debt of gratitude."[1] The addressee of Rudolf Steiner's letter, dated November 1890 and containing this excerpt, is neither his fatherly friend and patron Karl Julius Schröer, the Goethe expert and realist who believed in the propulsive force of ideas, nor the herb master Felix Koguzki, known for his spontaneous clairvoyance, whom Steiner would later on immortalize in his mystery dramas in the character Felix Balde. The addressee is Friedrich Eckstein, with whom Steiner had made friends during their time spent together as youths in Vienna. The singularity of this disclosure, as revealed in one of Steiner's letters at the turn of the century, parallels the unique nature of Friedrich Eckstein's own life. In what way did Steiner become "quite another per-

---

1. Rudolf Steiner, *Briefe Band II 1890–1925* (CW 30), p. 51.

son" in the aftermath of his encounter with Eckstein? *What did Eckstein mean to him?*

Let us first cast a glance at Eckstein's personality and at his development up to the momentous years of his friendship with Steiner. Friedrich Eckstein was born in Perchtoldsdorf near Vienna on February 17, 1861. Eckstein himself alludes to the event in a much less prosaic style. Shortly before he passed away, he wrote in his inestimable *Erinnerungen an alte, unnennbare Tage* [*Reminiscences of Unnamable Old Days*], "I was born into this world at the bottom of a deep, vast sea, whose blue tide then reached from the base of the Alps as far as Central Asia. Though—and this need be mentioned forthwith—this entire ocean had long since dried up a long, long time before I arose there."[2]

The "width of the sea" where Eckstein entered life equally enfolds him in the diversity, depth, and intensity of the influences he receives while in early childhood and adolescence. By the end of the 1870s, his father, a cosmopolitan, sociable man of great learning and a chemist by profession, had developed a new technique for producing parchment paper. He opened a factory that soon became a profitable and widely known enterprise. Early on his son becomes active as first "assistant" in his father's factory. He nearly loses his life one day during the explosion of a newly installed steam boiler. However, neither this nor other similarly perilous incidents deter him from taking over the factory later on at the age of twenty-one after his graduation. Already before entering Gymnasium Eckstein, highly gifted both intellectually

---

2. F. Eckstein, *Alte, unnennbare Tage, Erinnerungen aus siebzig Lehr- und Wanderjahren.*

and manually, pursues studies of chemistry and Latin under his father's guidance. Most of the time spent at the Gymnasium in Vienna, which he entered at the age of nine, just flies "past him with unbearable indifference."

Hence, he must turn to other spheres of life to quench his immense thirst for knowledge and satisfy his hunger for experience. He displays a great deal of interest in fencing; at the age of fifteen he is considered to be an absolute expert in this discipline. He studies Fichte, whose book *The Vocation of Man* had left a similarly lasting impression on Eckstein's father. Lorenz von Stein, a professor of public administration in Vienna, urged Eckstein to study Kant thoroughly, since his lack of knowledge of the latter's writings would render Hegel, Fichte and Schelling incomprehensible. Driven by a tremendous zeal, at the age of sixteen Eckstein plunges into the literary "ocean" of Goethe's writings. With breathtaking rapture he swims his way through the *Wilhelm Meister* novels from the first page to the last.

Around the same time he goes hiking and exploring nature, on his own or with friends, venturing forth into precarious climbing trips. In 1879 he ascends the Piz Bernina[3] "under tremendously difficult circumstances, unescorted by any guide, right through the middle of the maze of ice."[4]

At this point let us have a brief look at the spiritual signature of the aforesaid year, which inspires to daring ascents much more profound in nature. Rudolf Steiner's spiritual-scientific

---

3. The Piz Bernina, a mountain located near St. Moritz, Switzerland, with an elevation of 13,284 feet, is the fifth highest peak in the Alps.

4. Eckstein, op. cit.

reflections[5] reveal the workings of a real spirit-entity at the core of the so-called "zeitgeist," the guardian spirit of the age, which for a period of about 350 years bestows its spiritual impulses upon the era it inspires.

Michael—The Spirit of the Age

The new zeitgeist, since time immemorial called "Michael," ascends to the "throne" in 1879 after an "interlude" of rest following the age of Alexander the Great and followed by the reign of six other superseding guardian spirits. In the new era shaped by Michaelic impulses every human being is given the chance to prevail over the "ice labyrinth" of conceptual intellectuality—independently through his own efforts and without the authority of some leader—so as to gain free insight into the realm of actual spirituality. The "spiritualization of the intellect"—that is how Rudolf Steiner would subsequently come to describe this timely initiative to create a new awareness in the spirit of, and indeed called forth by, the reverberations of the new age. Conscientious consideration of the events of the day or simply the occasional reading of the daily newspapers and magazines should not be regarded as the principal criteria by which a modern man can be considered a true contemporary of his time. Rather, these manifest themselves in his capacity and willingness to grasp and assimilate the spiritual impulses of the prevailing "reigning" spirit of his epoch.

---

5. For Rudolf Steiner's theory of the sequence of the time spirits see lectures of May 18, 1913, July 19, and August 27, 1924. For more on the Michael Mission see *Anthroposophical Leading Thoughts* (CW 26).

Friendships

Impelled by his thirst for knowledge of all that is new and guided by his singular instinct for the fundamental impulses of his age, Eckstein climbs the Piz Bernina and by doing so he also ascends, so to speak, toward this new zeitgeist. How far, then, will he live and act according to the very spirit of his time? To what extent would he be guided by other, rather untimely forces?

In the autumn of the epochal year 1879 Eckstein attends seminars on mathematics at the Vienna Institute of Technology where he studies higher algebra and acquaints himself with projective geometry. He also studies mechanical engineering and attends lectures in chemistry, well prepared by the private lessons he received from his father. At the same time Rudolf Steiner takes up studies at the Institute of Technology. Here he encounters Schröer, whose patronage would be of great import to Steiner. As Eckstein later related to Edmund Schwab, who would often visit Schroer in the twilight of his life, it was he, Eckstein, who had introduced Steiner to Schröer. However, only five years later closer ties of friendship grew up between Steiner and Eckstein. It was essential that the common ground of their spheres of interest revealed itself first, so to speak. It always started with some area of interest enthusiastically explored by Eckstein that would then provide him with links to other, fellow enthusiasts. Thus it happened that several years earlier his enthusiasm for Goethe's *Wilhelm Meister* novels had earned him a friendship with Julius Mayreder. The latter had the intention of introducing Eckstein "to that strange soul, Rosa Obermayer, as soon as possible, thus betokening his gratitude for all my affection and confidence."[6] A bond of friendship was forged between Eckstein and her, later Rosa Mayreder, who would marry Julius's brother Karl and into whose circle of friends Eckstein would introduce his friend and "young Goethe devotee, Rudolf Steiner."

It also happened around the time of his first encounter with Steiner that Eckstein spontaneously struck up an intense friendship with the brilliant mathematician and natural scientist Oskar Simony. He chanced to meet him on a late summer day during a climbing trip. The two of them examine each other's collection of gathered herbs; at the top of the mountain, in a heated hut, they soon find themselves conversing about different issues of higher mathematics. "As I eventually realized," Eckstein writes in his recollections, "that my interlocutor had come to talk of Abel's integral equations, it suddenly flashed through my mind: 'Ha!' I exclaimed emphatically, 'now I see! You are going to introduce rational substitutions, which would possibly indicate the way to the rational axial lengths of the crystals?' 'Pretty good instinct!' exclaimed Simony, and with a vigorous slap on my shoulder he pulled me toward himself while bearing himself like an inebriate. That was the beginning of our long-lasting friendship."[7]

The two friends soon decide to meet weekly for "exchange courses." Eckstein comes every Monday morning to Simony to be instructed in the latter's "algebra of the higher manifolds"; whereas, Simony visits Eckstein each Thursday for a

---

6. F. Eckstein, *"Ein Gruß aus längst vergangenen Tagen"*; in *Der Aufstieg der Frau. Zu Rosa Mayreders 70. Geburtstag*, Jena, 1928.

7. Eckstein, *Alte, unnennbare Tage.*

privatissimum, or a lecture to a small group, on Descartes, Leibniz, and Kant's *Critique of Pure Reason.*

Yet Friedrich Eckstein was not only an outstanding mathematically and philosophically minded thinker. Not without reason was he born on the "seabed" of the so-called Vienna Basin, which acted in a way as a geologic–geographic magnet for numerous musical talents and geniuses, drawing them into the environs of Vienna. By the time of his first encounter with Simony, Eckstein was already a passionate devotee of Wagner. In July 1882, he went on a pilgrimage from Vienna to Bayreuth to the première of Wagner's *Parsifal.* There Eckstein mingled with the famous people of the day and even met Wagner personally. He is said to have later on bequeathed his pilgrim boots to the Wagner Museum.

Shortly before, he had met the then as yet less known composer Anton Bruckner. Eckstein passed many a precious moment in Bruckner's circle. Even so, his urgent and most ardent request for being accepted as a private student—Eckstein had already studied music theory for many years—Bruckner initially denied "in a most fierce, vehement, almost insulting manner,"[8] as we learn from Eckstein's *Recollections of Anton Bruckner.* The turning of the tide occurred later, in May 1884, while the "Wiener Stadttheater" is all ablaze; all of a sudden the two men's friendship acquires a new dimension. In the midst of the gaping crowd Bruckner suddenly seizes Eckstein by the arm and together they behold the sinister spectacle. Eventually they go to a nearby café to recover from the general turmoil. After a while Bruckner produces a piece of paper from his pocket with

---

8. F. Eckstein, *Erinnerungen an Anton Bruckner,* Vienna, 1923.

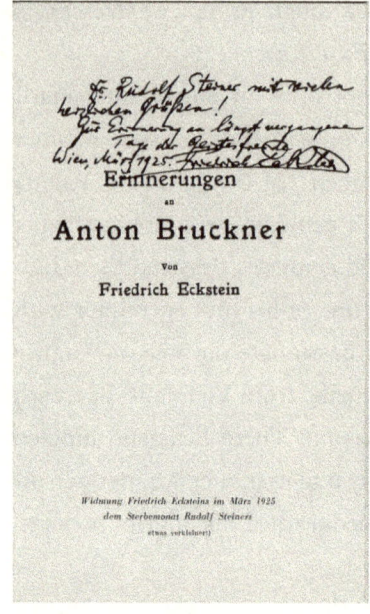

Widmung Friedrich Ecksteins im März 1925
dem Sterbemonat Rudolf Steiners
(etwas verkleinert)

a Latin hymn by Bernard of Clairvaux, which he intends to set to music. Bruckner reads out the first line and asks Eckstein whether he could translate the text for him, whereupon Eckstein recites the whole text from memory without a moment's hesitation and then translates it into German. Overwhelmed with the utmost awe and remembering that his friend had wished for private instruction, Bruckner invites Eckstein to come and see him the next day—the lessons are to be started forthwith.

During the years to come Eckstein accompanied Bruckner on his journeys, concluded publishing contracts on his friend's behalf, and arranged musical performances. In a word, he acted as a unique kind of private secretary. Sometime later he would smooth the way for Hugo Wolf in like manner.

Yet, let us once again turn our attention to the "course-couple" of Eckstein and Simony. Around the year 1883 the two friends became increasingly interested in the thriving Spiritism of that time. They paid close attention—albeit initially with thorough scepticism—to the experiments of the physicist and astronomer Friedrich Zöllner and the famous American medium Henry Slade.

Magicians and Theosophists

From the English physicist Lord Rayleigh, who at that time tarried in Vienna, the two friends learn of certain Indian "magicians" who could move objects through the air without employing any of the common physical means. Such phenomena were being intensely explored by the Theosophical Society that had not long before (1875) been founded by H.P. Blavatsky and Colonel Olcott. When Simony asked how it was possible for these Indians to perform such feats by sheer willpower, Rayleigh is said to have replied: "By the mere impact of spirits." To Eckstein they seemed "so peculiar, these accounts rendered by Lord Rayleigh," that he "promptly decided to approach the heads of the Theosophical Society."[9] He contacted the theosophist Franz Hartmann who had gone to see Blavatsky in India. Shortly afterward, in Vienna, Hartman moved in with Eckstein for a year. So the latter had direct access to information on the proceedings within the Theosophical Society. As early as 1884, the twenty-three-year-old Eckstein became "President of the Vienna Lodge" headquartered in Adyar/Madras. In 1885 the young head of the lodge received a message by telegram from Blavatsky's confidante saying: "If you want to see H.P.B. while she is alive, you must leave for Ostend at once."[10]

Eckstein arrived in Ostend at night, and after initially being met with opposition by two elderly ladies, he is eventually granted access to Blavatsky, although at a late hour. He finds her

---

9. See Eckstein, *Alte, unnennbare Tage*.

10. According to Robert Speiser, "Aus Rudolf Steiners Wiener Jahren." *Mitteilungen aus der anthroposophischen Arbeit in Deutschland*, Easter 1977.

sitting enthroned on her bed in the midst of a spectacular pile of cushions. They engage in a highly unconventional and inspiring conversation that leaves an indelible impression on Eckstein; the visit lasts five hours. At this point Eckstein and Steiner enter a phase of most intense dialogue. We learn from Eckstein's reminiscences: "Even in former days we had often met in the company of the famous Goethe expert, Prof. Karl Julius Schröer, and we'd had many a debate over Goethe's symbolism. In the meantime it had come to his attention that I was associating with leading members of the Theosophical Society and with Madame Blavatsky, who was very much a talking point at that time. Dr. Steiner impressed upon me his wish to learn more of these matters and asked me to initiate him into the 'Secret Doctrine.' That was the beginning of our regular correspondence that lasted for many years."[11]

During the period of his theosophical pursuits and studies Eckstein also worked on a remarkable natural philosophic essay, which appeared that very same year (1885) under the title *Compression Phenomena*. In the essay Eckstein endeavoured to examine the modern physical-atomistic theories from a philosophical perspective; with a keen eye he scrutinised some fundamental flaws inherent in those theories. What appears to be particularly revealing of his subsequent development is the manner in which he praised Kant as the great master of modern philosophy. Eckstein, the theosophist, seeks to "call attention upon" Kant's writings and to "urge" to a thorough study of them.

---

11. See Eckstein, *Alte, unnennbare Tage*. The *Secret Doctrine* (1886) is one of the two principal writings of H. P. Blavatsky.

A Friendship under the Guardian Spirit of the Age

Kant and Blavatsky? Within the realm of the human pursuit of knowledge one can hardly imagine more clashing opposites. What's more, whereas Blavatsky acts in the spirit of the new zeitgeist, in that she was the first to introduce spiritual lore into materialistic Western culture, quite the reverse is true of Kant's philosophy, which is literally a shield against the influences of the new zeitgeist. Kant questions and contests man's capacity for knowledge of occult phenomena. This Janus nature of Eckstein's spiritual aspirations poses a great riddle. In a way, it permeates the course of his life up to the very end.

Rudolf Steiner read his friend's paper, as a note on the copy in his private library shows.

During the years to come the two friends would regularly meet at the Café Griensteidl, which Eckstein liked to frequent, often in the company of Bruckner. Among the habitués of the Griensteidl were Hermann Bahr, Karl Kraus, Hugo Wolf, Rosa Mayreder and Stefan Zweig—to name only a few of the prolific personalities who contributed decisively to shaping the cultural scene in those days. "At certain times of the day," thus Steiner in retrospect portrays the life and activity in the Griensteidl, "it literally yielded a fragment of the Austrian literati scene."[12]

And what about the habitué Steiner himself? In the midst of all the "literati" in Griensteidl he sits working on his *Outline of a Theory of Knowledge based on Goethe's Conception of the World*. Whereas Eckstein engages in an apologia for Kant's abiding significance, at the adjacent table, so to speak,

---

12. R. Steiner, *Bildband 1: Die Jugendzeit Rudolf Steiners in Österreich*, with a biographical appendix by Wilhelm Rath (ed.).

sits Steiner with his foundational work seeking to deliver his contemporaries from their "unwholesome Kant-creed" and to illustrate the, as yet, inconceivable significance Goethe will have for the evolution of philosophical thinking in the ages to come. As one can imagine, this endeavour can hardly have ignited much enthusiasm in the Griensteidl circle. Many a polemic was presumably fuelled by the very question of the philosophic value of Goethe's world conception and its topicality as postulated by Steiner. Eckstein recalls heated controversies between Rudolf Steiner and Hermann Bahr, "and we always took great pleasure in listening to them whenever they were having a fierce argument, pouring forth streams of invective against one another.

"'Rudolf Steiner is incapable of following my thoughts,' Bahr once declared, 'since he is bogged down in his utterly antiquated, antediluvian ideas.'

"'On the contrary!' Steiner retorted, 'there's nothing easier for me than to comprehend Hermann Bahr of all people. All I need to do is to think back to the time when I hadn't learned anything yet!' This battle of words was accompanied by resounding laughter."[13]

In 1887 Friedrich Eckstein is introduced by Hugo Wolf to the home of Marie Lang and her spouse. Rudolf Steiner enters the same place only two years later, accompanied by Eckstein. He owes the most valuable impulses to his contact with this free-thinking, theosophically-minded circle, where he also meets Rosa Mayreder in spring 1890.

---

13. See Eckstein, *Alte, unnennbare Tage*.

"The Time Has Come!"

In the autumn of 1890 Rudolf Steiner moved to Weimar, where he had been summoned to edit Goethe's natural-scientific writings for the great Standard Edition [*Sophien Ausgabe*] of Goethe's works. Despite the prospect of significant and promising work waiting for him in Weimar, it was not easy for him to leave Vienna. In Weimar he did not find anything that could parallel the intense contacts he enjoyed within the Viennese circles. He resolved to temporarily forgo such impulses when he decided to take over the editor's task from Karl Julius Schröer, who did not feel qualified enough to work on Goethe's natural-scientific writings. Steiner was certainly also aware that his move would involve the risk of rupturing fine ties of friendship. The following statement, which he confides to his friend Eckstein in November 1890, affords a chance to gain insight into the frustrating effects attending his Weimar-decision: "You can hardly imagine how lonely and misunderstood I feel here. Since I left Vienna I have not yet had even one, single, sensible exchange of ideas with anybody."[14]

In the same letter he asks Eckstein, whom Steiner consults as an authority of undisputed competence, to give him "information, as soon as possible," on a passage from Goethe's *The Bride of Corinth*. "You surely know the symbolic meaning of salt and water." Eckstein's reply renders a subtle and extensive reflection on the symbolic purport of the items in question. For the symbolic implication of "water" he explicitly refers Steiner to "the ending of the fairy tale of the snake, where it drizzles in the dome of the temple." Steiner replies, promising his friend

---

14. See Steiner, *Briefe Band II,* page 29.

"interesting material" soon on the *Fairy Tale of the Green Snake and the Beautiful Lily*, to wit, interpretations from within Goethe's circles, gathered by the author himself. At that point Steiner himself hadn't yet had the opportunity to review them.

The passages quoted from their letters do not really convey the impression that the two friends had not exchanged thoughts on the *Fairy Tale* before 1890. Wilhelm Rath presumes that it was also Friedrich Eckstein who inspired Steiner toward an intense study of *The Fairy Tale*. Be that as it may, the fact that Steiner and Eckstein discussed not only Goethean symbolism in general, but also Goethe's *Fairy Tale* in particular, may hold the key to one of the most significant components of their friendship.

The imagery of Goethe's *Fairy Tale* clearly signifies a watershed long overdue in humanity's history of the occult. The secret temple of age-old knowledge of the occult was to be raised out of the concealed nether reaches, whereto only few had been able to find the way into the bright light of the day—fully visible to every seeking soul. "The time has come"—thus cries out the Old Man with the lamp three times, always master of the circumstances, thereby ushering in the revelation of the temple and its secrets.

Peregrinations into the Occult

Time and again Rudolf Steiner explains how the events in the *Fairy Tale* parallel the real, spiritual course of events—the suprasensory preparation for the guidance by the zeitgeist of the new age, the Archangel Michael. In the autumn of 1879 Goethe's *Fairy Tale* formula is called upon by the new spirit of the times to come into force. According to Steiner's spiritual research, since this epochal autumn "the time has come" to render accessible the occult truths veiled by the mist of symbolism. These very truths—hitherto shrouded in mystery and handed down in obedience to the strictest precautionary measures—must be made accessible, along with the supernatural facts of humankind that were initially explored by Steiner himself. Steiner devoted himself to this revelation-impulse in his endeavour to convert occult facts into abstract concepts, or, to use an image from Goethe's *Fairy Tale*, to convert them into the "coin of the earth." For it is but in the shape of this "coin" that, in the age of intellectuality, those facts will be grasped through common sense by every person and then conveyed to the general public. Steiner often characterized the *Fairy Tale* as a "miniature" of this grand promulgation and transformation-impulse.[15] It is no accident that Steiner prefaced his public spiritual-scientific activity with a lecture given in Berlin on Michaelmas 1900 on Goethe's *Fairy Tale*. He once described that Michaelmas lecture as the "cradle" of the entire subsequent development of the Anthroposophic movement![16]

As profound as was Eckstein's knowledge of the *Fairy Tale*'s symbolism, just as weak proved his ability to absorb its real, spiritual background. He was denied this insight by his Kantianism, perhaps also by some deep-seated convictions conditioned by certain karmic elements. If we picture Friedrich Eckstein as a further character in Goethe's *Fairy Tale*, we would find him vociferously crying out against the Old Man with the lamp: No, the time hath not come yet!

---

15. For instance, on July 8, 1924, in Dornach.

16. On Sept. 25, 1920, in the speech on the eve before the opening of the first anthroposophic academic course at the Goetheanum.

In one of the January 1925 issues of *The Goetheanum* (today found in *Autobiography*) Rudolf Steiner gives an account of the "not really unchallenging resolutions" attending the "public disclosure of the knowledge that Anthroposophy encompasses, i.e. the knowledge of the spiritual world." The main difficulty with divulging this spiritual wealth resided in the circumstance that Steiner was confronted with an army of those cognoscenti who had a wide knowledge of the original spirit-cognition that was veiled in symbolic guise and for which they demanded that it be kept in strict secrecy even in the modern age. He portrays Friedrich Eckstein as such an authority of the "old guard," while aware that he himself owes many valuable insights to Eckstein.

> When I knew him he did not write much, but what he wrote was full of spirit. Yet, at first no one would sense from his writings that he was an intimate who knew of the ancient spiritual knowledge. This is active in the background of his spiritual work.... Eckstein vigorously maintained that esoteric knowledge of spirit should not be made available publicly as we do ordinary knowledge....
>
> Friedrich Eckstein believed that one who is "initiated" into ancient knowledge should invest what is said publicly with the power gained from such "initiation." Esoteric knowledge itself, however, should be kept strictly apart from exoteric knowledge—that is, esoteric knowl edge should be reserved for a limited circle of people who are able to fully understand its value.
>
> In order to become active publicly on behalf of spiritual knowledge, I had to make the decision to break with this tradition.[17]

---

17. R. Steiner, *Autobiography: Chapters in the Course of My Life, 1861–1907* (CW 28), p. 200.

Thus, we find the real reason why they came to part company toward the turn of the century in the spiritual distance that arose between these two friends, rather than in the physical distance created by Steiner's moves to Weimar and Berlin. Yet, even after the turn of the century there are at least two further encounters between them, which makes it obvious that, despite their wide "esoteric discrepancy," certain elements in their friendship proved to be unwavering.

Mysterious Conversion

By the time Steiner left Vienna in late autumn 1890, Eckstein seems to have undergone a most bewildering change—some of his friends considered it alarming, indeed. On September 10, 1891, Steiner wrote to Rosa Mayreder, who had obviously informed him of certain incidents that had occurred, giving expression to his "utter distress" at Eckstein's evolution. He, Steiner, had known for long "that Eckstein was going fatally astray in that he took the phrase 'You must enjoy life to the full' quantitatively, as though it meant that you should haphazardly enter into whatever comes your way, however trivial or shallow the experience may be.... I, too, believe that the true man of knowledge must fully absorb the substance of life and the universe in all its manifestations. Yet, it is imperative that this happen qualitatively through an ever-increasing deepening, rather than by wandering about through every imaginable experience.... People of knowledge must experience everything, however, by seeking it in the right place and not by waiting until the experience imposes itself on them randomly. Friedrich Eckstein doesn't know this and therein lies the tragic doom enveloping this truly grand and significant personality...."[18]

Toward the end of the 1890s, Eckstein resigns his theosophical office and converts from Judaism to Protestantism. In April 1898 he marries Bertha Helene Diener, thirteen years his junior, who is a creative, somewhat eccentric, woman coming from a middle-class family. The young couple, to whom a child is born in the following year, moves to Baden near Vienna. There Eckstein sets up a private library, which in later years would comprise about 16,000 volumes. At first his young spouse follows him with devotion on his spiritual peregrinations into the lands of mysticism and occultism. Her own talent flames up and stirs her passion for literary creativity. Yet, in the long run, her "spiritual haven" turns into "spiritual captivity." Her talent lies dormant. During this time Eckstein travels; whenever he is back in Vienna, he turns up at the Café Imperial, his new residence since the closure of the Griensteidl in 1897. There he converses or corresponds with diverse personalities, such as Mark Twain, Thomas A. Edison and Sigmund Freud to name a few and who have hitherto gone unmentioned. In February 1907 Rudolf Steiner delivers two lectures in Vienna: one for the members of the Theosophical Society; the other, a public lecture titled *Knowledge of the Suprasensory in Our Times and Its Meaning for the World of Today.*[19] Eckstein mingles with the audience. A few years before his death he relates to Edmund Schwab how he perceived Steiner

---

18. See Steiner, *Briefe Band II,* p. 115.
19. The only reported lecture of Steiner's in Vienna in February 1907 was on February 22 to members of the Theosophical Society. The public lecture mentioned in this article is, to date, unreported in the CW.

at that time: "He said he had been horrified; Steiner seemed to be out of his mind, talking incredible nonsense."[20]

The Ecksteins divorce in 1909. Freed from "spiritual captivity," Bertha Eckstein-Diener devotes herself to literature. During the following decades she publishes numerous articles, essays and novels under the *nom de plume* Sir Galahad, which remained for a long time veiled in secrecy. *Mothers and Amazons* is one of her works that is still known today.[21]

As regards Eckstein, he "sits enthroned" more and more frequently in the Imperial and is, for the most part, highly honoured as a polymath; at times he is even ridiculed. Karl Kraus, for instance, once spread the following satirical-fictitious anecdote about him: "Last night I had a nightmare...: a Brockhaus-volume[22] descended from the shelf to look up something in Mac Eck." [23]

Around 1913 there followed another encounter with Steiner. The two friends arranged to meet at the Café Landmann near the Burgtheater. As was often the case in the '90s, they again focus their attention on an intricate Goethe-passage. Eckstein wants Steiner to interpret the passage from Goethe's poem *The Mysteries*, which revolves around a shield revealing a bear that

---

20. Edmund Schwab, "Aus meinen Erinnerungen an Friedrich Eckstein." *Blätter für Anthroposophie*, vol. 1953, pp. 178ff.

21. See also Sibylle Mulot-Déri, *Sir Galahad*, Frankfurt, 1987.

22. *Brockhaus Enzyklopädie* was a German language encyclopedia published by Brockhaus.

23. Quoted after R. Fülöp-Miller, "Der Narr im Frack. Auf den Spuren von Dostojewskis nachgelassenen Schriften." *Der Monat*, no. 46, July 1952. "Mac Eck" is an abbreviation of the way Eckstein often signed his letters: *Machtiger Eck*. See, for example, *Briefe Band II*, p. 31.

holds a bleeding arm between his jaws. According to Edmund Schwab's notes, their conversation in the Landmann went as follows: "Tell me, do you believe in the existence of masters?" enquires Steiner first off. Eckstein replies: "But you were once my student and have yourself experienced some master-inspirations as humbug." Whereupon Steiner observes: "That's a shame. Well, in that case, there's nothing left for me to tell you either." Thereupon Eckstein concludes: "That's most unfortunate. I have been unable to interpret it up till now—and I didn't deem it worth bothering with. I surely can go on dispensing with it altogether." Yet, Eckstein continued to maintain his interest in Steiner's personal development and work, above all "turning his attention to...his mystery dramas, yet without gaining any confident or approving attitude toward his work."[24]

Literary Activities

During the war years Eckstein studies the latest literature from Ireland. He translates essays by W. B. Yeats, which appear in the Insel Press in 1916 and are prefaced by him. He studies the Bohemian Brothers and edits a work by Amos Comenius on this significant brotherhood, likewise prefaced by himself. Some of Eckstein's reflections in those prefaces still betray the "spirit-alpinist"—for instance, when he writes in reference to Yeats:

> The highest spiritual force knows no contentment or fulfilment; it is preordained to find "no place to rest." It is destined to leave behind all that is attainable, all the things on earth, as though they were but a symbol of eternity. Its wistful gaze is fastened on the infinite distances "beyond existence," beyond the fading points of all creation. In such

---

24. E. Schwab, "Aus meinen Erinnerungen an Friedrich Eckstein."

"soaring of the soul" and its love of eternity, in its boundless transcendence of all existence, there resides the highest dignity and value of man.

Together with René Fülöp-Miller, the author of *The Power and Secret of the Jesuits*, Eckstein, generously investing the financial resources at his disposal, acquires the German publication rights to a significant part of Dostoyevsky's literary legacy. In the mid-twenties the first volumes edited by Eckstein and Fülöp-Miller are published at the Piper Press.

At the beginning of 1925 the mathematician Ernst Blümel draws Eckstein's attention to Steiner's essay in *The Goetheanum* (mentioned above) where the latter commemorates his friend from his youth. Eckstein is most enthusiastic about it. Upon hearing of Steiner's critical illness he is strangely affected. On March 6, Eckstein sends his erstwhile friend a copy of his previously published book on Bruckner along with a written dedication and a cover letter in which he enthusiastically pays homage to the time spent together in their youth. Steiner is said to have replied in like manner with fond affection. However, the thank-you note mentioned by Eckstein could unfortunately not be found to date.

The Last Years

Eckstein's subsequent path will be but briefly précised here. It deserves its own, separate essay, as the mysterious character of this "grand and significant personality" is altogether worthy of an ample biographical appraisal.

The occupation of Austria had put a sudden end to the gatherings of Jewish intellectuals and artists at the Café Imperial. Shortly afterward the "Führer" himself resided at the hotel, which bore the name of the coffeehouse to which it belonged. Years before, Eckstein had once said to Ernst Müller with reference to the then leading politicians: "You can hardly imagine what level these people are at!" And on another occasion he bitterly remarked that "Russia was the only cultural state left in Europe."[25]

On November 10, 1939, shortly after the outbreak of World War II, Friedrich Eckstein died in Vienna of pneumonia. Throughout his life Friedrich Eckstein had an exceptionally self-confident nature. His handwriting, no less than his habit of heavily underlining his own signature, bears witness to it. He was endowed with a brilliant memory and a broad intellect. As one of the cognoscenti of the ancient spiritual wisdom he was, as it were, a treasure trove of occult knowledge for his friend Steiner. Thanks to his exoterically—i.e. by literary-historical means—pursued researches in the sphere of the occult, Eckstein undoubtedly spared Steiner many a laborious and time-consuming detour. For that, and presumably for reasons more unfathomable, Rudolf Steiner had, in a most specific way, expressed his thanks to him in the very letter that formed the starting point of our essay. However, it may well have been precisely this erstwhile "master-pupil" relationship that denied Eckstein the capacity to grasp and appreciate with the requisite objectivity the ever increasing spiritual calibre of his friend.

Retrospectives and Prospects

In his Weimar letter of November 1890 Rudolf Steiner spoke of his two most profound biographical-altering occurrences.

---

25. Ernst Müller, "Erinnerungen an Friedrich Eckstein." *Blätter für Anthroposophie*, vol. 1950, pp. 418ff.

"About one of them I will remain silent," he wrote to Eckstein. What remarkable wording, for whoever resolves to *absolutely* keep silent about a thing, will not speak about that very silence, either. Did he mean to let Eckstein, his "master," know that he would well be able to fathom, by means of independent thinking or by indirect approximating queries, the fact that even at the close of the nineteenth century there were still significant initiates acting in secrecy? Did he want Eckstein to understand that whatever "humbug" concerning so-called occult masters they may have been up to within the theosophical movement was of minor importance? For, it is beyond doubt that in mentioning that *first* occurrence, Rudolf Steiner is alluding to his own encounter with an initiate-individuality who acts with complete anonymity. In the autumn of 1907 Édouard Schuré, whose spiritual insight was unencumbered by any "Kant haze" and who had no doubts about the existence of great master-individualities, had the opportunity to find out concrete details about this deeply altering encounter. [26]

Eckstein's studies of mathematics and philosophy had taught him what pure conceptual and sense-freed thinking meant. Yet although it is certain that he had occasionally passed beyond the "ice labyrinth" of conceptual intellectuality, he could gain no access to genuine spiritual insight, at least not into such fundamental spheres of real spiritual phenomena as were stirring the new zeitgeist in 1879.

---

26. See Édouard Schuré in his introduction to the French translation of *Christianity as Mystical Fact*; Contributions to *Rudolf Steiner Gesamtausgabe*, summer 1973. See also T. H. Meyer, *Rudolf Steiner's Core Mission*.

"Many an...abyss, many a treacherous rock have I passed; many a thick haze has clouded my view," is the symbolic self-confession we read in Eckstein's reminiscences. "Yet, from many a laboriously surmounted height was I granted a soothing prospect, and fresh hope was bestowed upon me...By virtue of my being close to many great personalities, my faith in humanity and in its infinite purpose...has been confirmed and has grown stronger." Among these "great personalities" his friend Rudolf Steiner counts not the least, of whom Eckstein renders a portrayal—albeit not an extensive one—in his reminiscences. Still, is it conceivable that his encounter with Steiner would not be reflected after Eckstein's death in the further activity of this "significant personality"?

Ploughing, sowing, reaping—these are the natural stages in the evolution of every single individuality, and they apply to interpersonal relations as well. Have the seeds of friendship between Rudolf Steiner and Friedrich Eckstein already fully sprouted? If not, they are "destined" to come up in future cycles of evolution.

THE TWELVE WORLDVIEWS AND ANTHROPOSOPHY

WITH A FOCUS ON ANTHROPOMORPHISM

> Thus the developing human "I,"
> Forgetting itself and
> Mindful of its origins,
> Speaks to the Cosmic All:
> If I can free myself
> From the chains of personality
> I will fathom my essential being
> In You
>
> *Calendar of the Soul*
> Third week (April 21–27)

Dear Friends,

We have just heard a verse from the *Calendar of the Soul* that fits perfectly with our theme for today. I hope this will become clear during the course of my talk. The subject of this lecture encompasses the twelve worldviews, with their seven moods and three tones, and then concludes with the most important element connected with the worldviews—namely *Anthropomorphism*.[1]

---

1. Wikipedia describes *Anthropomorphism* as a term coined in the mid-1700s to refer to any attribution of human characteristics (or characteristics assumed to belong only to humans) to non-human animals or non-living things, phenomena,

As we heard in the verse, freeing oneself from the bounds of self is a concept that is also valid when considering the one-sidedness of worldviews. The one-sidedness of a worldview does not originate with our higher being, but from our subjective personality; we might also say it originates from our lower self or lower "ego." We can make a concrete effort to acknowledge our peculiarities in the form of one-sidedness and overcome them in this arena of worldviews and their moods.

I would like to begin with a quote by Egon Friedell that was submitted by a reader of the *Der Europäer*[2]: "One should not ask a thinker *which* point of view he or she has, but *how many* points of view one has. In other words, is that person's mental apparatus extensive or is it narrowly focused?" This

---

material states and objects or abstract concepts, such as god(s). Examples include animals and plants and forces of nature such as winds, rain or the sun depicted as creatures with human motivations, and/or the abilities to reason and converse. The term derives from the combination of the Greek ἄνθρωπος (*ánthrōpos*), "human" and μορφή (*morphē*), "shape" or "form." The precise use Rudolf Steiner makes of this word is elaborated beginning on page 134. —ED.

2. *Der Europäer:* About 25 years ago, T. H. Meyer discovered the anthroposophic monthly journal *The Present Age,* edited by Walter Johannes Stein and published in London in the 1930s, prior to the outbreak of World War II. This led to his intention of founding a similar periodical for our time. He was able to fulfill this intention after he finished his biography, *Ludwig Count Polzer-Hoditz: A European* (1869–1945) ("Ludwig Graf Polzer Hoditz—Ein Europäer"). Polzer was involved in the question of the future of Europe, which has become such a burning issue today, to almost a greater extent than all of his contemporaries. On this basis, and with the help of a number of further contributors, the first issue of the monthly journal *Der Europäer* ("The European: Symptomatic Events in Politics, Cultural Life and the Economy, Monthly Journal on the Basis of Rudolf Steiner's Spiritual Science") was published in November 1996.

The Twelve Worldviews and Anthroposophy

statement was made by Friedell in his book *Quarry*,[3] in the chapter "What is Truth?"

Now we must encounter a basic prerequisite for all worldviews. A thinker should not develop only one distinct point of view, but instead should strive for a variety of worldviews.

Each thinker—and we are all thinkers—wants to find a worldview. Rudolf Steiner showed us that there are, in principle, twelve worldviews, twelve doors into reality, so to speak. Each point of view seeks out what is true or real from its own perspective.

Rudolf Steiner gave the essential spiritual-scientific lectures on this theme in *Human and Cosmic Thought*[4] half a year before the start of World War I. This cycle of lectures was another attempt to contribute to peace among nations.[5] To contemplate and work with the twelve worldviews and achieve mobility with them, to let go of the longing to hold onto and represent only one point of view, is a subject closely connected with the question: how is it possible to achieve peace among human beings? It is intrinsic in human nature to represent one-sided views that can be argued, even if it might be enough to understand the other person's point of view. It makes no sense to argue a point of view. It is more meaningful to ask if the point of view is the best one for a certain situation. One-sidedness in worldviews leads to habitual, repetitive action.

---

3. *Steinbruch, Vermischte Meinungen Und Sprüche*, Nabu Press (February 22, 2010).

4. *Human and Cosmic Thought*, Jan. 1914 (CW 151).

5. Steiner's lecture cycle *The Mission of the Folk-Souls In Relation to Teutonic Mythology*, June 1910 (CW 121) also contributes to an understanding about the differences between peoples.

Rudolf Steiner wanted to give an impulse for versatility and universality in thinking. Naturally, he did not intend to stimulate vague concepts, but to stimulate sharp, clear thinking that, at the same time, becomes mobile.

Mobility in Thinking

With the following example, Rudolf Steiner makes clear what he means by mobility in thinking.

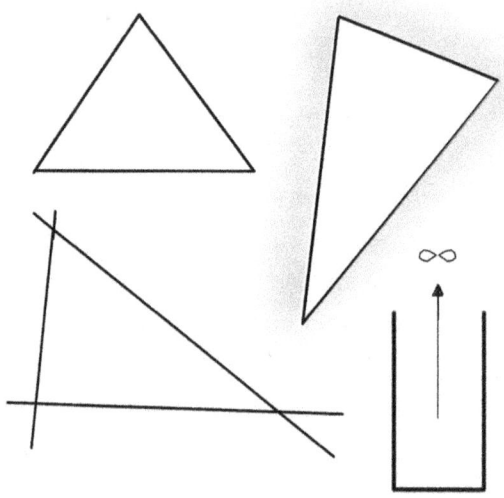

I refer to this example because it is essential for all that follows. The example is taken from geometry, which no one argues about today.

All of the figures are triangles, although none of them is THE triangle. Even the example with one angle set at infinity can be considered a triangle. All of the shapes have the same lawfulness as their source. This is the lawfulness of THE triangle, the concept of "triangle." The archetypal triangle, in contrast to the single triangular shapes, is invisible and can only be perceived in thought.

Now we should bring all of the individual triangular shapes into movement in such a way that they go into each other, so that one metamorphoses into the other very quickly, in all directions. This is an example of mobility in thinking based on the same lawfulness.

We should apply this exercise to our theme of twelve worldviews! We have to become as mobile when we move through the twelve worldviews as we did when we worked with the triangles.

Journey through the Twelve Worldviews

Worldviews are like twelve monumental doorways into reality. I want to briefly characterize them for you with an easy example—namely, the hall here where we are gathered.

We can, indeed, think of something as trivial as this hall from twelve different points of view.

I will start with **Realism**, a technical term for the worldview we will now apply to this hall. All that is around us, all that we can see around us, is "real." As realists, in this sense, we see things everywhere: rows of chairs, a flight of stairs, participants and the lecturer.

Someone can say it is too vague for me to speak only of "objects." I want look at the objects more specifically. I will focus on them. Then I look specifically at the objects as phenomena. This term commands a certain respect. A phenomenon is an accurately delineated thing you can focus on. It has contour and form. It becomes interesting for science. Things are sufficient for daily use; the scientist researches phenomena. There is a reason that this expression is important in Goetheanism and

Anthroposophy. We look at objects, but when we research them they have to become phenomena. Thus, I see not only objects but also phenomena; the people present here are obviously included. This point of view is called **Phenomenalism**.

Now let us continue and say that objects and phenomena are all well and good, although we principally deal in reality with what our senses perceive. Without the senses nothing of what is around us would be there. You notice that when the lecturer speaks too softly you cannot hear what is said very well. We are considering sense perception and move from the appearance (the phenomenon) to the starting place of the senses that perceive it. **Sensualism** is the name of this worldview. The entire spiritual-scientific doctrine of the senses belongs here. As you know, there are twelve senses. Here we must always ask: with which senses do we perceive something? It's not always easy to answer this question. You might say, for example, with the spiritual-scientific–sensualistic approach of reading a book, that the sense of thought is active. This is not the case. I will come back to this point later.

We will now leave the point of view of Sensualism and carry on. We can also be of the opinion that something is not an object, or a phenomenon, or a sense perception but is something that is material and visible. From Sensualism we take with us, at most, the sense of touch, which gives us an experience of "matter"—**Materialism**. Reality is only the chair I sit on, my body that I can feel, my neighbor whom I can touch if I want to. Beyond those points the unreal begins.

Of course there are mixtures of the various viewpoints. People exist who strive for the spirit where they see something real (in a pure form this would lead to Spiritism). At the same time, however, they want the spirit to be something tangible. They believe in spirit and spirits when they can appear materially to them. Table lifting, knocking signs and the hearing of voices and so on are examples of this view. *Spiritism* is a bastard lying between **Materialism** and **Spiritism.**

Perhaps some of the audience will now say everything presented as real up to now is not *my* reality. For me, it is all about the thought, the idea of something. For example, what is the *purpose* of this hall, in addition to all of the things inside? Someone else might say it is a movie theatre. We are able to come here and see movies. Naturally, all members present will immediately correct this and say that it was once a movie theater, but now serves anthroposophic lectures and events. Then one might ask if it has been properly built for that purpose. You see, this leads to a different worldview, one that Steiner calls **Rationalism,** where thoughts are realized and embodied in something.

In our enthusiasm we skipped a point of view from which this next question originates. Not only thoughts are embodied here and, although we continue to count with ideas, we are dealing strictly with numbers. When you look at this hall from this perspective your first concern is: how many people are here? How many of those who are usually here are not here now? What did a ticket cost? How many minutes will the speaker go overtime? This is reality for the worldview of **Mathematism.** Everything that can be counted, weighed and calculated is real here. This point of view, like all the others, also has its rightful place. I have to practice mathematics when I pay my bill in a restaurant, otherwise I wouldn't notice that the waiter made a mistake and the amount of the bill is too high. All viewpoints need to be considered equally. Nevertheless, one must also ask which areas of life are best served by a particular point of view.

Now let's move on from simple ideas (numbers) and from rational ideas (Rationalism), which we have already discussed, to the next worldview. Aren't there ideas that go much deeper and have not been realized, yet are nonetheless real? Such ideas we can call *ideals*. That is what one calls real from the worldview of **Idealism**.

A person could call Idealism an "elevated rationalism" when following the thought movement from rationalism. You see, it is important to move from a concrete train of thought to the neighboring, or to an opposing, point of view. A rigid definition of a viewpoint doesn't work, for example, when I want to define one triangle located next to the other without making the necessary transition. This is what was explored with the example of the hall.

Now that we have arrived at Idealism, we can ask ourselves how we got here from Rationalism. We got here by seeking more in the world than what has already been realized. Unrealized ideals, for example, those of a moral nature, are much more real for me. If one does not seek *more*, one does not get beyond Rationalism. This process, this transition that we just went through, is the essence, is the factor that brings us into movement. If you now look around as an idealist you may ask if there are ideals here, and not only ideas with a purpose. Naturally, you have to answer: of course! All anthroposophical lectures are filled with them.

Now we can go still further and say that ideas and ideals are not hovering in the air. They must be connected with beings; they need carriers, they need souls. Now the ideas and ideals are no longer the reality but the location where they manifest is, namely, the soul. One differentiates no further than this and labels everything that carries ideas as soul. The reality is the soul that carries the ideas. Rudolf Steiner calls this point of view **Psychism,** a widespread view today.

After a while this view can become somewhat uncomfortable. When the audience and the lecturer only look at each other from the viewpoint of Psychism one could imagine that the group soul of the hall is thinking.[6]

It is not easy to take this point of view in a gathering of anthroposophists. Individual consciousness, which is so strongly developed in everyone present here, is overlooked. In addition, there can be a need not only to be a soul (even when the soul thinks and has high ideals) but to be something more substantial, like *spirit*. Soul is a moving ocean; spirit is the rock within it. With this we have made the step to **Pneumatism.** Consequently, as a pneumatist, I say to myself that spirit is also found here in the hall, not only soul. Again, there could be people who want to go further because spirit is too vague and unsatisfactory, even after a certain firmness was achieved through Pneumatism.

Having accepted the spirit and also a conscious awareness of one's own individuality, the demand is for more spirits—plural—spiritual beings, including one's own spiritual individuality. This is **Spiritism.** There exists a whole world of spirits, hierarchies of spirits...and the human spirit is one of them.

---

6. A real spiritual group soul is not meant here.

We would like to know how many individual spirits are present here when we look into the hall simultaneously from the viewpoint of Spiritism and Mathematism. The relation between Anthroposophy and Spiritism is evident; but, as we will see, they are in no way equal.

The difference between Pneumatism and Spiritism is explained by Rudolf Steiner using a wonderful example. What you see in the distance as a swarm of mosquitoes is, when close up, perceived to be a world of single beings. This is the advancement from Pneumatism to Spiritism, an approach to individual spirit beings.

Let's go on. It can be exhausting to continuously look into the world of individual spiritual beings with their ideas, deeds and sufferings. By throwing a veil over them we retain one of their qualities, that of imaginative beings having different levels of consciousness. Each object in itself is an enclosed imagining being. This view is called **Monadism.** So, all of the objects here—the lectern, the chairs and walls—all correspond to different stages of conscious representations. It is not a very widespread worldview but it can be very fruitful for human poetic talent. I'll read a short poem to you that will bring this view to expression:

> *Sleeps a song in things abounding*
> *that keeps dreaming to be heard:*
> *Earth's tunes will start resounding*
> *if you find the magic word.*

This is how Joseph Eichendorff honored the poetic spirit of monadism. You might say you can recover from the reality of Spiritism with Monadism and create poetry. What could be the

The Twelve Worldviews and Anthroposophy

story of a shoe! A shoe, taken off at a mosque after its owner finally arrives in Mecca, will relate how it suffered from the feet that moved it along.

A less poetic spirit might ask: How can you call that real? Reality is something totally different for me—and today this is widespread—the energy in the world that streams out of things is real. Where you find energy you find reality. When looking at the personalities here in the hall one could ask where the energetic and strong people are. Who radiates dynamically? Many people today believe that dynamism already indicates the importance of a personality. Again, this is very one-sided thinking! It is known that many people have been seduced by great human dynamos who led them into the abyss. This point of view is called **Dynamism.** It is found everywhere today, and where it is one-sided can be very misleading. Imagine where Dynamism could lead when it is connected or mixed with Materialism, Psychism or Spiritism.

The drawing on the following page shows the relationship between the worldviews and the signs of the zodiac, which will not be further discussed here. Only so much needs to be said. We are dealing here with a spiritual realm that goes beyond astrology, which we will also see later with the worldview moods and the planets. You cannot decide on a person's dominant worldview merely from the position of the Sun in their birth chart.

Of course, we can now practice (not only here in the hall) finding the twelve worldviews in all directions in order to obtain mobility in the many contrasting views by leaving one and exchanging it for another. Just as we moved with triangles through various formations, we must be able to move freely

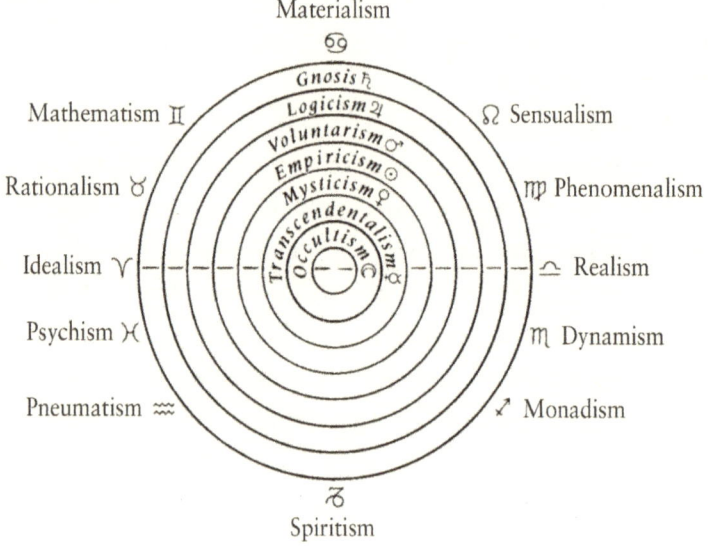

between these worldviews. This will lead to clear and mobile thinking. Our thinking will become rigid and narrow if it is clear but immobile. It threatens to become blurred if it is mobile and unclear. Both qualities have to be connected.

For now, let us remember that all these points of view give us something with which to know reality. None of the twelve views is unjustified or superfluous. In the unfolding of history you will see in the foreground one or the other worldview. Materialism was less widespread in the past than it is today. Phenomenalism already played a great role in the old mysteries and is today the best foundation for scientific research of the sensible and suprasensory worlds. Currently Realism, Dynamism and Mathematism are in the foreground. You will find some Psychism and Pneumatism in all spiritual movements that are still frightened by a concrete spiritual world. It is important to understand that the twelve indications have specific meanings and should not be understood in an associative manner. For example, in the past Realism meant about the same thing that we call Idealism today. For the philosophers in the Middle Ages the *idea* was the most important and they called the idea *Realism.*

The Seven Worldview Moods

Now we will consider what Rudolf Steiner called the seven worldview moods. The expression *mood* already indicates that we are moving into the realm of soul. The twelve worldview moods or nuances of worldviews, as they are also called by Rudolf Steiner, exhibit more of a spiritual character. We are descending from the zodiac into the region of the planets. We undergo a process of contraction and are a little less cosmic than before. We become planetarians. Look at how they become differentiated. A worldview dives down into one or another worldview mood. You can be a realist in seven different ways, although most often, only in one way. I will provide an example of this. But, before I do, I will list the planetary moods. We first arrive in the Saturn sphere in the worldview mood of **Gnosis**; then, in the Jupiter sphere we experience the mood of **Logicism**; in the Mars sphere, the mood of **Voluntarism**; in the Sun sphere, the mood of **Empiricism**; in the Venus sphere, the mood of **Mysticism**; in the Mercury sphere, the mood of **Transcendentalism**; and finally, in the Moon sphere we come to the mood of **Occultism**. Again, this is a list of specific expressions that are only meant to be used and understood in a specific context. See the above figure.

Let us start again and take this hall as we did before from the viewpoint of Realism. I will limit myself to what I see when

I look at this space and what is around me. Soberly, I register what I see without a specific soul condition. I speak simply of the things that show themselves to me. In this instance I am in the mood of **Empiricism.** I can also say that this is too easy. What I see in the hall reveals itself to me only when I put myself in a mood of fathoming or understanding. Only then can the true content and character of the things in the hall be revealed to me. I make a great effort and give myself the time until it starts to dawn on me where I am and what is around me. This is the mood of **Gnosis.** Perhaps this mood is easier to grasp when we choose a sacred space with plenty of things to discover.

You might also want to experience the thought of this space. This is not the same as realizing the purpose of the hall (the viewpoint of Rationalism). You want to experience what the sense of this space is in relation to the world-all, not only in relation to itself or to the town it is in. This is the mood of **Logicism.** Someone could now say: "I will do something different. I will sit down and wait until I experience inwardly the reality of the space and the things in it." In this state you enter the **Mysticism** mood regarding the hall. This is not something anthroposophical gatherings should strive for, no matter what viewpoint you take. Doing so could easily lead the soul into a fog where the audience would begin to have inner experiences that would have less and less to do with what the lecturer is attempting to convey.

Now, someone else comes along and senses a variety of forces (**Voluntarism**). Another person would like to walk up directly to the walls of the hall and knock on them. That person sees many objects and people but thinks what is real is hidden behind these things, behind something like a big Spanish wall. In this way we can experience Realism in the mood of **Trancendentalism**. Reality lies *behind* everything. When you are a character like Hamlet, you break through a wall somewhere and catch the eavesdropper Polonius.

With the mood of Transcendentalism something else is always found behind the wall; reality comes toward me, but stops behind the Spanish wall.

Finally, someone in the mood of **Occultism** can look around this space and say: "There is nothing to see; it's all maya. There is no reality here for the eye!" Such would be Realism in the mood of Occultism.

Now imagine that this hall is suddenly transformed into a picture gallery where we would like to see a particular picture. Perhaps by using this model we can get a little closer to the moods. This is an example that Rudolf Steiner offered and then developed using the mood of Gnosis. He says the following. "There are also people who are especially illuminated by the worldview of Realism. They go through the world in such a way that their whole mode of perceiving and encountering the world enables them to say much, very much, to others about the world. They are neither spiritualists nor idealists. They are quite ordinary realists. They are equipped to have fine perceptions of the external reality around them and about the intrinsic quality of things. They are highly sensitive to the qualities of things. They are Gnostics, genuine Gnostics, only they are Gnostics of Realism, and such Gnostics of Realism, and spiritualists or idealists [or anthroposophists] are often not Gnostics of Realism at all. We can, indeed, find that people who call themselves good theosophists may go through a picture gallery and have nothing to say about it, while others who are not theosophists at all, but are Gnostics of Realism, are able to say an abundance of meaningful things because with their whole personality they are in touch with the things they see. Again, how many theosophists go out into the country and are unable to grasp with their whole souls anything of greatness and sublimity of nature. They are not Gnostics of Realism."[7]

Let us stay for a while with the picture gallery. A Gnostic of Realism would definitely not rush through the gallery. Let us assume that such a person has decided to look at some pictures. Instead of simply going from one picture to the next, the Gnostic of Realism would stay with each picture for a long time in order to penetrate it deeply, again and again. Afterward, this observer can describe exactly what has been seen.

A person looking at a picture in the mood of Logicism will soon ask about the picture's meaning. What is the meaning of this painting and how does it relate to the whole creative work of the painter? The logician always goes for the whole while relating all details about it. What thought is carried by the painting, what is its deeper meaning? The person in a mood of Logicism sees thoughts everywhere in the world. Hegel was one of the greatest logicians of all time. To him, everything was thought; everything was an objective fabric of thought. Sense perception was also a form of thought for him.

A person looking at a picture in the mood of Voluntarism immediately asks about its effect. This person asks, what does

---

7. *Human and Cosmic Thought*, lect. 3

this picture want from me? It repels or attracts me. To look at a picture in this way is, again, a completely different mood of Realism.

In the empiricist mood, the observer stands before a painting in a matter-of-fact way and, with little effort, simply registers what is observed. The empiricist may not consider that altered lighting could cause the picture to make a different impression. The empiricist also can describe what has been seen very well.

The mystic takes his time. He waits for the picture to speak. This person wants the picture to reveal something inwardly, whereas the Gnostic wants time to engage and delve deeply into the picture. We also hear these words in the *Calendar of the Soul* verse. The mystic lets the picture be revealed through inner, contemplative silence. The mystic approaches the picture with a pure, inner mood of devotion. In modern galleries, one will often not get that chance. There (in modern galleries), the mystic does not easily get a feeling that something can be revealed. For example, the mystic looks at Joseph Beuys's *Fettecke* (a social sculpture constructed of five kilograms of butter). The empiricist could be very interested in this item because it is a new experience—and the empiricist is after experiences.

As a transcendentalist, I ask myself: What is behind the picture? This scenario is depicted in Rudolf Steiner's first *Mystery Drama,* in which Strader wants to cut through a portrait to find what it is that fascinates and to discover what is behind it. The picture hides something from me—its essence.

Now, when I go through the gallery as a realist in the mood of Occultism, then something very different must come out of the experience. I do not want to cut through the canvas to reach its essence, as the transcendentalist might do. The occultist will say that the reality of the picture is not visible at all. That could also be true for the painter. Painters can feel that their painting has nothing to do with what was in their mind. This may happen especially when depicting a soul with spiritual content. Nothing of it appeared on the canvas! The painter can, in this way, experience an occult mood for one's own creation. Then the painter tries again or gives up. The painter may persist and not give up—perhaps by changing the mood of Realism so that the thought can be achieved.

All seven moods are valuable, though we find that certain moods are more common than others. I believe the Gnostic mood from our verse—of delving deeply—is not very common today, not even in people with spiritual aspirations. A passive intake of spirituality is widespread—for example, a three-week course to become enlightened, or visits to a clairvoyant or reincarnation therapist. At best, we find a mood of Mysticism brought to spirituality. Before one can bring a Gnostic mood to spirituality, one will need to overcome the common laziness in thinking. A one-sided transcendentalist mood can also be found; its one-sidedness, which suspects that everywhere something lies behind, can lead to a distrust of the world.

The Gnostic mood was still widespread at the time of the Mystery of Golgotha and through subsequent centuries. Sooner or later one has to become a Gnostic again through the study of Spiritual Science, because Anthroposophy demands the will to penetrate deeply into a subject.

The Twelve Worldviews and Anthroposophy

Of course, today, the mood of Empiricism is widespread. For better or worse, it is the mood for practicing science, both natural and Spiritual Science. Initially, it is about taking in what can be experienced soberly and unemotionally in space from the realm of forces or ideas or from the world of the hierarchies (Spiritism). The mood of Empiricism was characteristic for Goethe, and, of course, for Steiner. Thus, Steiner gives the example of the important fact of thinking and the being of thinking as an experience he calls a "higher experience amidst other experiences."

If, in contrast, you approach thinking in a mood of Transcendentalism, you can lose your focus as soon as Transcendentalism starts to dominate. One searches everywhere for something that is truly experienced behind thinking, and the searcher could become blind to the thinking itself. Steiner has demonstrated that especially with regard to thinking one has to remain a naive empiricist because it confirms the beingness of the thinking experience. Whoever believes that the essence of thinking and all else in the world is behind the appearances, and who therewith develops this mood to the extreme, moves in the direction of Kant's view. Kant says there is one reality—the thing-in-itself that human thought cannot reach; it reaches only as far as the appearance of things. And the thing-in-itself, its true reality, remains forever hidden behind the Spanish wall of appearances.

Although Steiner does not say it explicitly, in my opinion it is obvious that Kant arrives at his conclusion by going too far into the worldview mood of Transcendentalism. You might say he has isolated this mood from the other six, elevated it to a theory, and made it an absolute.

Once again we see, as with the twelve worldviews, that the important thing is to learn to move from one mood into another.

In a certain way, Occultism is much more of a daily phenomenon than it would seem at first. When you read a book, for example, it is often possible to believe that thoughts are found in it. Yes, but please tell me where are these thoughts? Are they on the paper, in the paper or in the letters? When reading, we treat what we have before us entirely in the mood of Occultism: the letters as such do not exist. No one who reads is interested in what he actually sees . . . all those dark symbols on paper. Once having learned how to read, a person can make a jump from what is seen to what is completely invisible, that is, the meaning and the thoughts of what is being read. Whoever learns to read the "book of nature" in this mood goes about it in the same way, not specifically, but generally . . . only the "letters" are more complex. Everything becomes "a letter" in the big book of the world. Reading is a mysterious happening!

A child, as yet unable to read, must think it extremely curious that adults can look for hours at these papers with black characters, all looking the same, without getting bored. As mentioned before, in the view of Sensualism—also among anthroposophical friends—the opinion that we are aided in reading by the *sense of thought* does not hold up under closer inspection. (We use the sense of sight in reading and if we are blind, the sense of touch.) Anthroposophist and thinker Hans Bornsen[8] has pointed out how we form words and sentences while reading, and then think about those words and

---

8. Hans Börnsen, *Vom Lesen Im Buche der Natur*, p. 22.

sentences to find the meaning in what we have read. This is different from what happens when we are listening. The listener can indeed perceive thoughts in and behind the words with his sense of thought.

Becoming Versatile in the Worldviews and Moods

Once we have worked through the basic structure of the twelve worldviews with their seven nuances, our understanding can become fruitful for many other things. Deeply penetrating the lecture cycle *Human and Cosmic Thought* through a Gnostic fathoming does not occur by reading it once, but by reading it many times. I want to illustrate this with Rudolf Steiner's own words. In the above-mentioned lecture cycle, after having sketched the twelve worldviews and seven moods, Rudolf Steiner says: "Broadmindedness is all too seldom sought after. Anyone really in earnest about truth would have to be able to represent the twelve shades of world-outlook in his soul. He would have to know, in terms of his own experience, what it means to be a Gnostic, a Logician, a Voluntarist, an Empiricist, a Mystic, a Transcendentalist or an Occultist.[9] All this must be gone through experimentally by anyone who wants to penetrate into the secrets of the universe according to the ideas of Spiritual Science. Even if what you find in the book *How to Know Higher Worlds* does not exactly fit in with this account [given in *Human and Cosmic Thought*], it is really depicted only from other points of view and can lead us

---

9. By the term *occultist* Steiner here means a human being who lives in the worldview mood of occultism, not in the specific sense of a spiritual researcher. The earlier example regarding reading indicates that we are all occultists in this sense.

into the single moods that are here designated as the Gnosis mood, the Jupiter mood, and so on."[10]

Three examples of Worldview Moods in How to Know Higher Worlds

Rudolf Steiner doesn't become more explicit about the worldview moods in *How to Know Higher Worlds*, but if you look for them they can be found. I want to read a superb example of the Gnosis mood from this well-known book of instruction. This mood already makes itself known in the first sentence.

"There slumber in all human beings faculties by means of which they can acquire for themselves knowledge of higher worlds. Mystics, Gnostics, Theosophists—all speak of a world of soul and spirit that, for them, is just as real as the world we see with our physical eyes and touch with our physical hands. At every moment, the listener may say: what they talk about, I, too, can learn if I develop within myself certain powers that today still slumber within me."

This is the Gnostic mood in its purest form. Even when Rudolf Steiner mentions Mystic here in the beginning it is Mystic in the sense of the Gnostic mood: an active fathoming, an awakening of slumbering faculties. You know you have to do certain things in preparation before the object of higher experience can reveal itself to you. That is how, in *How to Know Higher Worlds,* willing readers are advised to prepare themselves for this Gnostic mood of knowledge. Perhaps the meaning of this mood becomes clearer than it was in the example of the picture gallery. (One must use complex and difficult pictures. It

---

10. *Human and Cosmic Thought*, lect. 3.

The Twelve Worldviews and Anthroposophy

is difficult to get into a Gnostic mood with the lines of a Mondrian picture, for example.) This instruction book is also an appeal to the other seven moods of knowledge. Searching systematically, one can probably find all seven moods in its pages. For instance, the mood of Logicism is found in places where the discussion is about the objective reality of thoughts. We will now consider two more moods:

> Only if we surrender ourselves repeatedly to a particular thought, making it completely our own, can we achieve anything. This thought is: "I must do everything I can for the education of my soul and spirit; but I will wait calmly until the higher powers consider me worthy of illumination."[11]

I suppose it is not too difficult to recognize the two moods indicated here. To begin with, practice every activity you can by consciously developing spiritual strength for inner life, which is the mood of Voluntarism. The polar opposite is quietly waiting, devotionally, for spiritual illumination, which is the mood of the mystic.

The mood of Voluntarism can make clear the necessity for developing inner forces. If it is missing, then the reason for practicing remains veiled. One might find that, through practice, something subjective comes into their experience. This demonstrates the importance of "experimenting" with all the moods, as Steiner says, to become clear about your preference for one or the other, so you can overcome that singularity.

Almost all of the great creative achievements from the past are based on human striving for specific knowledge, although

---

11. *How to Know Higher Worlds*, p. 84.

in the future it will be important to develop universality. Spiritual science is like a watershed between these two tendencies of spiritual development. To demand universality is one of the most important tasks of Anthroposophy and one of the reasons behind the lecture cycle that my talk is based upon.

Hegel was great through his one-sided Logicism and that is how, according to Steiner, he became "the greatest philosopher of the world." Philosophy mainly deals with thought. Leibniz, whose thoughts were not poetic but practical, leads one to the art of engineering and tunnel building. His thought became great through Monadism. Kant drove Transcendentalism to its unproductive extreme.

In the future all one-sidedness has to become unproductive. When you discover that you have an overdose of the mood of Empiricism you should not build a matter of fact worldview upon it but, instead, seek to develop the mystic or occult mood, which is not easy.

Examples of Cognitive One-sidedness and its Conquest in the Mystery Dramas

In the mystery dramas we see people who suffer from one-sidedness and how they are able, more or less, to overcome it. Their whole path of development is colored by a one-sided cognitive attitude. I'll give an example from the third scene in the fourth drama: a character (I will provide the name later so I don't give it away to those who know it) says:

> To strive for nought—but just to live in peace,
> Expectancy the soul's whole inner life:
> That is the mystic mood.

The Twelve Worldviews and Anthroposophy

It is Felix Balde who speaks in this mood of Mysticism in Venus. It is the basic mood through all of his incarnations, from the time when he functioned as Guardian of the Threshold in the Egyptian Temple. Already at that time, he was silent and able to wait. In the same scene we see another character in another mood in a very interesting way. This character hears Felix Balde and his friend Capesius saying things that were often heard before and believed to have been completely understood. Suddenly there arises with the same words a totally different experience. He says:

> I often understood your present speech—
> And then I thought it wise—but not a word
> In all your speech can I now understand.

Now for us comes the crucial sentence for what we are trying to accomplish here:

> Capesius and father Felix both
> *Conceal dark meanings in transparent words...*[12]

Every word is exactly as it is printed. It is not a "dark" meaning expressed in "dark" or "vague" words, but a "dark" meaning in clear "transparent" words. Rudolf Steiner comments on this scene in a lecture given in Munich on August 24, 1913. He is not explicit about which mood is speaking, but with a little Gnostic mood we can find it ourselves. He says:

> O, if only a good number of our friends could put themselves into this mood of expectation! If only they could adopt this frame of mind, of awaiting the approach of something whose description in advance, both as theories and

---

12. Emphasis added.

as explanations, has apparently been clear enough and yet misunderstood—then something would take place in their souls that is expressed by Strader's words in Scene Three of *The Souls' Awakening*. Strader stands there between Felix Balde and Capesius, stands there in a remarkable way—he stands there so that he literally hears every word they say and could repeat it, and yet he cannot understand it. He knows what it is, can even consider it to be wisdom, but now he notices that there is something that can be expressed in the words: Capesius and Felix, both...to me...conceal dark meaning in transparent words.[13]

Then Steiner points to the present:

Our supremely clever people today will perhaps concede that, by chance, this or that person can hide meaning—clear meaning—in obscure words. However, it will not easily be granted by these clever people that an obscure meaning can be hidden in clear words." And now comes the point: "*Nevertheless for human nature to concede that in clear words an obscure meaning may be hidden is the higher acknowledgment of the two.*[14]

Through this clear recommendation, a cognitive mood is given that we already know. A cognitive mood, when not exaggerated, can be very productive for the crossing or the transcending of the threshold of knowledge. And that is what we all seek! Who does not know the moments when, after repeated study, all clear words are really clear, which means they are truly understood? This feeling, however, will not last long. Who isn't also familiar with the experience that occurs when one has reached the limits of cognitive stagnation? At this point one has

---

13. *Secrets of the Threshold;* Aug. 24, 1913, lect. 1.
14. Ibid., emphasis added.

The Twelve Worldviews and Anthroposophy

no further questions. In this situation, a dose of transcendentalist mood will be healing and bring progress.

This is also what happens with Strader. An inner cognitive process arises from a place of obtuseness. He truly approaches the threshold of the spiritual world and is able to see the abyss that opens between the sense-perceptible and the spiritual worlds. Later, in a mood of Gnosticism, he fathoms the depths of his experience. We meet him in earlier situations as a human being who carries more of the mood of Empiricism. This is remarkably universal compared to Felix Balde's mood of Mysticism. Here we see Strader suddenly enter the mood of Transcendentalism. Something long known to him suddenly becomes a question. This mood of questioning something that is "clear," yet not clear, is what moves him forward.

In Anthroposophy, we know the great value of questioning. Today, however, we live in an answering-culture. Even with regard to profound political events like the attacks on September 11, 2001, we must not ask! There is almost no place for Transcendentalism, except in the exaggerated and therefore unproductive manner of Kant. We need, more than ever, truly balanced Transcendentalism, harmonized with the other moods. We cannot make cognitive progress if it is lacking.

How can one truly understand Steiner's basic philosophical works without insight into the language of philosophical Idealism, revealing that they are spiritual experiences? This shift was advised to the young Rudolf Steiner by one of his master teachers. When you have understood these works, the question can arise: how do they fit into the total development of Rudolf Steiner?

Real knowledge never ends. Transcendentalism is the great teacher of this insight. There is a reason it is connected with Mercury, the messenger of the gods. It dissolves the limits of cognition. If you want to develop this you will...after reading the same lines seventy-eight times...then suddenly you may have a new insight.

Three Tones of Sun, Moon and Earth

After all this the elements that belong to the worldviews are not yet exhausted. We must also look at the so-called worldview tones and Empiricism.

The three tones are treated, at best, like orphans in the secondary anthroposophic literature. Literature exists about the twelve worldviews (Sigismund von Gleich,[15] later Mario Betti[16]). A lesser amount of literature exists on the seven moods (von Gleich[17]). The literature is silent about the so-called tones. That is why it is justified to address them in brief. They are connected with the earthly relationship the human being has to the sun and the moon. We might have the inclination to look for the source of life and spirit in the sun or to look on earth for what is illumined by the sun. Or, we might prefer to walk the world in the light of the moon, preferably the full moon. Rudolf Steiner calls these three tones, and they can be both a worldview and a worldview mood: *Theism, Naturalism and Intuitism*. Just imagine the complexity that can now unfold! It is possible for someone to have a

---

15. S. von Gleich, *Die Wahrheit als Gesamtumfang aller Weltansichten*.

16. M. Betti, *Zwolf Wege, die Welt zu verstehen*.

17. Von Gleich, op. cit.

The Twelve Worldviews and Anthroposophy

base tone of Theism but, at the same time, to be a materialist with regards to their worldview. This person might develop an inquiring, almost worshipping, adoration of matter. Ultimately, matter originates in spirit, which is also the view of Spiritual Science. A materialist with a theistic base tone could find Anthroposophy interesting; this is less so for someone with a naturalistic base tone. Such persons would have no ear for the spiritual origin of matter; for them it is merely nature. They look only at what is illuminated, not at the light source itself; they have the sun at their back, so to speak. Intuitism has a greater presence in the realm of fantasy and creativity. In the moonlight things receive life and spirit as sharp outlines vanish. Imagine someone is a monadist ("Sleeps a song in things abounding") and also an intuitist. Perhaps Christian Morgenstern had something of this combination when he wrote his humoresques. It is easy to recognize that the three tones are related to a triad that played a great part in humanity's inner development and will do so again in the future. They connect with the triad of art, religion and science.

At one time they were harmoniously related, then they separated from each other, and in the future they will come again into harmony through Spiritual Science.

A forerunner of future Universalism, where all three tones were working together, can be seen in Goethe. "He who possesses art and science has religion," he once said. People are most often inclined toward one of the worldview tones. Also, in relation to worldviews and worldview moods we could find that Goethe embodied a wide variety. As a scientist, he was a phenomenalist. But was he not also a spiritualist, a pneumatist, and an idealist as well? And did he not have a mood of Empiricism as well as Mysticism, yes, even the mood of Gnosticism and other moods, not to speak of Transcendentalism?

Anthropomorphism

I come now to the last component of Steiner's worldviews: Anthropomorphism. It is perhaps the most difficult to understand. It can be easily misunderstood if you see only its trivial side, which Steiner points out himself. He makes it possible to misunderstand and misjudge the deeper meaning of Anthropomorphism very easily by saying: In addition to the three tones there is something else. It comes about when human being take as a starting point what they find within them.[18] This is the "next and also most trivial" worldview component. It is correct but not complete. Perhaps Steiner wanted to leave this up to the reader's mood of Transcendentalism, Gnosis or even to his anthropomorphic faculty of cognition. He always counted on his readers to work out all the parts that are between the lines.

To understand Anthropomorphism better, let us take the following expressions of Steiner from one of his earliest writings.

> The essential nature of a thing thus comes to light only in relation to the human being. The essential being of each thing appears only for human beings. This forms the basis for relativism as a worldview; a trend of thought that assumes that we see all things in the light that the human being lends to them. This view also bears the name anthropomorphism, which has many representatives. Most of these, however, believe that this peculiarity of our cognition alienates us from objectivity as it is, in and of itself. We perceive everything, so they believe, through the spectacles

---

18. *Human and Cosmic Thought*, lect. 3.

> of subjectivity. Our worldview shows us the exact opposite. If we want to reach the essential nature of things, we must view them through these spectacles. The world is not merely known to us as it appears, but rather appears as it is, though only to contemplative thinking.[19]

This is not the trivial side of Anthropomorphism, rather the cognitive science of its essential side. Through cognitive inspection the essence of things are revealed to the human being. A person has only to start with himself by focusing inwardly and becoming active as a thinking being. Otherwise, the only result will be projections of the part of the self that is not thinking. This is the crucial point of Anthropomorphism and the basis for its ambivalence. How do I take hold of myself and what do I find in myself? Do I find only the most trivial things, products of my heredity or hereditary traits, a wide range of sensations, or do I find something higher, such as thinking?

And yet, just before the end of his life, in the First Class lectures Steiner characterizes Anthropomorphism without naming it explicitly. "All of these things by themselves can provide the ground for the fundamental discovery that human beings need on their path of knowledge, plumbing the depths of their own self [the mood of Gnosticism], wherein the universe has, after all, planted the sum total of its secrets so that they can all be found out of the very self, in the self-knowledge of the human being. Here will be found all that people need, both in days of health and in days of illness, on the path of life between birth and death, and that one will also need to apply on that other

---

19. *Goethe's Theory of Knowledge,* pp. 60–61.

path of existence between death and a new birth."[20] This is Anthropomorphism in its deepest and broadest sense.

Review and Preview

We began with twelve worldviews, came to seven moods, then to three tones, and have now arrived at the most trivial, but also the deepest and, in a certain sense, the most important of all: Anthropomorphism. As we have heard, there one asks: What reality can I find in the world starting with what I find in myself? Cosmologically this represents the earthly human being strictly by himself, without regard to the Sun or Moon. Naturally, this can become trivial when I cannot go beyond my "ego." When I only find the ego in myself, and perhaps overstate this ego and call this exaggeration my reality, the only possible result is illusion. If I can find something deeper in my humanness, however, then I can rise from this depth to the three tones, to the seven moods and finally to the twelve worldviews. I will speak about these depths in a moment. Take it provisionally for now.

We have come from the periphery, over the planets to what is in the end only a point, where we have only the point of our own self. Now we will try from this point (Anthropomorphism) to rise up again to the heights of the spiritual cosmos. How can the point become a circle? That is the next question. Or even more precisely, what exactly in the point can become a circle? The point can, indeed, become a circle when I can grasp what is already of cosmic origin within it, and this comes from the periphery. The element that leads us out of point consciousness

---

20. *DerMeditationsweg der Michaelschule*; Feb. 15, 1924 (cw 241 a–c).

has been characterized by Steiner in all his basic works as thinking. I find thinking in myself; when I learn to cognize thinking I will see that its being originates not in myself, but that it has its own independent being. One can continue and ask: What is this being of thinking by itself?

Rudolf Steiner has been asked this question. In the last chapter of *The Philosophy of Freedom,* it is said that thinking is a "primordial being" that all people take hold of when they think. It is "the common primordial being" of all thinking people. When we carry in our thinking a real spiritual being that only appears when we think, then we can in consciousness through thinking rise from the point to the periphery of the cosmos. When Walter Johannes Stein asked Steiner about the primordial being of thinking, Steiner said, "It is the oldest of all the Archai, sort of like a group soul of humanity, which today is destined to become a Spirit of Form."[21] Perhaps it is the only acceptable group soul of humanity because of its compatibility with individual freedom and activity. We can find through the method of Anthropomorphism a high spiritual being connected with our thinking activity that is essential for all cognitive activity, as we have discussed tonight. This is how thinking, insofar as it is connected with a distinct Archai being, can lead us into the world of hierarchies. Thus, far from where we have descended we rise again in the spiritual cosmos from where we started. This aspect of *The Philosophy of Freedom,* which leads into a spiritual world inhabited by spiritual beings, is also explained in the following quotation. It comes from a conversa-

---

21. W. J. Stein and R. Steiner, *Dokumentation eines wegweisenden Zusammenwirkens,* T. Meyer (ed.), Dornach, 1985, p. 284.

tion between Rudolf Steiner and Walter Johannes Stein. "When you wrote *The Philosophy of Freedom*," Stein asks, "were you already conscious of the hierarchies you wrote about in *An Outline of Esoteric Science* and other works?"

"I was conscious of them," answered Rudolf Steiner, "but the language I spoke at the time had no way of formulating it. That came later. Through *The Philosophy of Freedom*, the human being rises to perceive the human as a spiritual being. Although this is described in *The Philosophy of Freedom*, it is true that, by engaging actively in the experience of freedom, the human being finds the hierarchies in the perceived spiritual environment of the spiritual human being because they are all in the human being. The spiritual environment of the human being is visible to spiritual vision. That is why they are not formulated in *The Philosophy of Freedom*, though they are there."[22]

This is how, through Anthropomorphism, we can get from the core of thinking out and up to the spheres of the hierarchies. In this way we come into the realm where one of the twelve worldviews is most suitable: Spiritism, best supported by the mood of Gnosticism. Now we are back to Spiritism, while we started with a phenomenon right in front of us: thinking in its cosmic, hierarchical aspect. However obvious this anthropomorphic path into the spiritual cosmos may seem, it is often overlooked because we imagine the spirit always in the far distance. The spirit of thinking is not only close to the thinker, but in thinking the "I" unites with it and can, therefore, enter the spirit of the cosmos, although at

---

22. Stein and Steiner, op. cit., p. 299.

first this only appears in the form of ideas. But ideas are substantially no different than spirit, just as ice is substantially no different than water. This is how the activity of thinking gives us the start and possibility to reach our higher self, and through it, to reach the world of the hierarchies. The caricature of such Anthropomorphism at its best and deepest sense would be one's own lower self that is not thinking. Even leaving Rudolf Steiner's spirituality far below one's self, it is possible to deny and inflate it into a cosmos. A short illustration of this danger can be seen in the following example. A former Waldorf student and current journalist wrote recently: "We pass the ranks of gods.... We can take pride in our progress, because we did it ourselves. We humans are brilliant, and to prove otherwise would not serve the world.... When God is awakened through our waking up, when our consciousness is God's awareness, then the spiritual realm, the origin of all ideas where Steiner drew his experiences from, is less broad and luminous than the realm where we draw our inspiration from. God is awakened through our awakening." This is also Anthropomorphism, but here the highest was not attained, although all sorts of murkiness and arrogant conceit are puffed up as divine. Or, in another example, "there is only one energy."[23] Clearly, the writer has an affinity to Dynamism, perhaps also to Voluntarism. "In the past I thought there were many different energies. But recently I had ample experience that, in reality, there is only one energy." This road leads from moderate narrow-mindedness to serious narrow-mindedness, from many forces to only one force!

---

23. Sebastian Gronbach; see *Der Europäer,* March 2008.

Protean Anthropomorphism and the Anthroposophic Path of Knowledge

Where does social life fit in with all that we have discussed today? Rudolf Steiner says "the worst enemies of truth are the closed and finite worldviews that want to erect a world structure in a few thoughts." All is energy, all is force, and so on.

"The world is boundless, both qualitatively and quantitatively. It will be a blessing when there are individual souls who wish for clear vision with regard to what appears in our day with such terrible, overwhelming narrow-mindedness, and wants to be universal."[24]

When we move inwardly through views, moods, and tones and are eventually able to grasp the true meaning of Anthropomorphism, we find protean truth in it, a real key to the versatility needed to overcome one-sidedness. *Starting with Anthropomorphism, one can experience all the tones and all the moods in all of the worldviews.*

To achieve this aim one has to regard the true spiritual nature in the human being; one cannot remain with their physical or soul natures. The resultant anthropomorphic path of knowledge in Anthroposophy leads back again to the spiritual cosmos from where we originate.

For reasons of clarity, let me conclude by answering a question that may have already answered itself. Is Anthroposophy one of the twelve worldviews? Of course not! It could perhaps be regarded closest to Spiritism. And yet, it may not be identified with Spiritism alone or with any other worldview. It is something much deeper. It is what arises when one descends

---

24. *Human and Cosmic Thought*, lect. 4.

into the spiritual depths of one's own being. From that place the path leads out and up again through the worldview tones, moods and nuances. Thus, starting from the point of Anthropomorphism, we can become a sphere again, with a mobility that can protect us from one-sidedness. In this way understanding is developed for each worldview, which promotes peace. Greater understanding will be developed about the difficulty of freeing oneself from single worldviews and moods. I need not remind you that we speak of moods of knowledge, not of some emotional mood of which there are surely more than seven.

The new edition of *Human and Cosmic Thought* by Archiati Publishing is titled *Twelve Worldviews* and subtitled *and Seven Moods of Soul*. This is misleading and could attract people who are more interested in moods by themselves than in specific cognitive moods.

Anthroposophy as an anthropomorphic, cognitive path leads us away from a point out into the world of the spiritual hierarchies and their deeds. We can roughly describe what we have discussed here today as a lemniscate, double path, going from the periphery inward, then through the eye of the needle of thinking and out again into the periphery.

In conclusion, let us listen to the "clear" well-known words of Rudolf Steiner in a new light considering our contemplations tonight, especially with regards to the deeper functions of Anthropomorphism. I mean the words of Rudolf Steiner from his legendary *Leading Thoughts*. The first leading thought provides, "Anthroposophy is a path of knowledge that would like to guide the spiritual in the *human being* to the spiritual in the universe."[25]

---

25. *Anthropsophical Leading Thoughts*; Feb. 17, 1924 (cw 26).

Representative Men

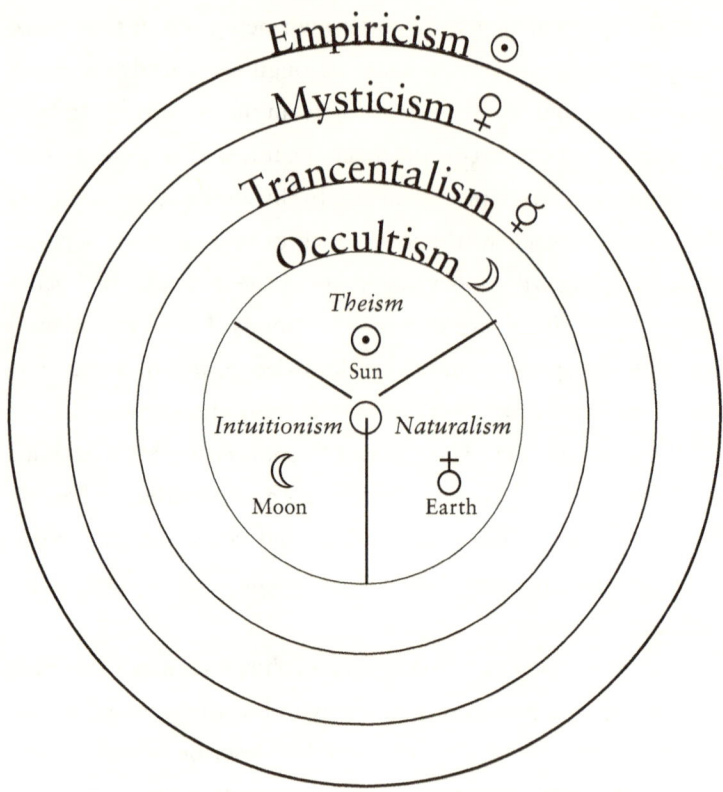

CITED WORKS

Bernoulli, Carl Albrecht. *Nietzsche und die Schweiz*. Leipzig, 1922.

Betti, Mario. *Zwolf Wege, die Welt zu verstehen*. Stuttgart, 2001.

Binder, Hartmut. *Kafkas Welt—Eine Lebensgeschichte in Bildern*. Hamburg, 2008.

Börnsen, Hans. *Vom Lesen Im Buche der Natur*. Dornach, 1985.

Brod, Max. *Der andere Rudolf Steiner*. Dornach, 2005.

Burdach, Konrad. *Faust und Moses. Records of the Prussian Academy of Sciences*. Berlin, 1912.

Dunlop, Daniel N. "Seelenläuterung durch Leid—Das Beispiel Oscar Wildes." In: *Der Europäer*. April 2008.

Eckermann, Johann Peter. *Conversations of Goethe with Johann Peter Eckermann*. New York: Da Capo Press, 1998.

Eckstein, Friedrich. *Alte, unnennbare Tage, Erinnerungen aus siebzig Lehr- und Wanderjahren*. Vienna, 1936.

Frenzel, Ivo. *Friedrich Nietzsche: An Illustrated Biography*. Cambridge, UK: Pegasus, 1967.

Funke, Peter. *Oscar Wilde*. Hamburg: Rororo Monographie, 19th ed., June 2006.

Gershom, Rabbi Yonassan. *Are Holocaust Victims Returning?* Dornach, 1997.

Gimpel, Georg. *Weil der Boden selbst hier brennt, Aus dem Prager Salon der Berta Fanta (1865–1918)*. Prague, 2000.

Goethe, Johann Wolfgang von. *West–East Divan: Poems with "Notes and Essays"* (trans. M. Bidney). Albany: SUNY, 2010.

Hoffmann, David-Marc. *Rudolf Steiner und das Nietzsche-Archiv*. Dornach: Rudolf Steiner Verlag, 1993.

Janouch, Gustav. *Conversations with Kafka,* 2nd ed. New York: New Directions, 1971.

Kafka, Franz. *Briefe an Ottla und die Familie*. Frankfurt, 1975.

———. *Tagebücher 1909–1912,* 3rd ed. Frankfurt, 2000.

Karlén, Barbro. *And the Wolves Howled: Fragments of Two Lifetimes*. London: Clairview, 2000.

Meyer, Rudolf. *Goethe—Der Heide und der Christ*. Stuttgart, 1965

Meyer, T. H. *D. N. Dunlop: A Man of Our Time*. London: Temple Lodge, 1992.

———. "Die *Erdenkrankheit an der Wurzel fassen...*"—*Eine aphoristische Betrachtung* über die Inspiration als Zukunftsfähigkeit des Menschen, in Laurence Oliphant, *Wenn ein Stein ins Rollen kommt*. Basel, 2004 ("Attacking the Earth Malady at its Root"; in *When a Stone Begins to Roll;* see Oliphant below).

———. *Rudolf Steiner's Core Mission: The Birth and Development of Spiritual-Scientific Karma Research*. London: Temple Lodge, 2010.

———. *Wegmarken im Leben Rudolf Steiners und in der Entwicklung der Anthroposophie*. Basel, 2012.

Nietzsche, Friedrich. *The Complete Works of Friedrich Nietzsche*. Palo Alto, CA: Stanford University Press, 1995–2012.

———. *The Gay Science* (trans. Walter Kaufmann). New York: Vintage, 1974.

———. *Sämtliche Werke, Kritische Studienausgabe in 15 Bänden*. Munich.

———. *Thus Spoke Zarathustra* (trans. R. J. Hollingdale). London: Penguin, 1969.

Oliphant, Laurence. *When a Stone Begins to Roll: Notes of an Adventurer, Diplomat & Mystic: Extracts from* Episodes in a Life of Adventure (T. H. Meyer, ed.). Great Barrington, MA: Lindisfarne Books, 2011.

Raabe, Paul. *Spaziergänge durch Nietzsches Sils-Maria*. Zürich, 6th ed., 2005.

Steiner, Rudolf. *Anthroposophical Leading Thoughts: Anthroposophy as a Path of Knowledge: The Michael Mystery*. London: Rudolf Steiner Press, 1998.

———. *Aus der Akasha-Forschung, Das Fünfte Evangelium*. Lecture, Dec. 10 (CW 148).

———. *Autobiography: Chapters in the Course of My Life, 1861–1907*. Great Barrington, MA: SteinerBooks, 2006; previously *The Course of My Life*. London: Rudolf Steiner Press, 1986.

———. *Esoteric Lessons 1910–1912: From the Esoteric School*, vol. 2. Great Barrington, MA: SteinerBooks, 2012.

———. *Four Mystery Dramas*. Great Barrington, MA: SteinerBooks, 2007.

———. *Friedrich Nietzsche: A Fighter for Freedom*. Blauvelt, NY: Garber, 1985.

———. *Goethe's Theory of Knowledge: An Outline of the Epistemology of His Worldview*. Great Barrington, MA: SteinerBooks, 2008.

———. *How to Know Higher Worlds: A Modern Path of Initiation*. Hudson, NY: Anthroposophic Press, 1994.

———. *Human and Cosmic Thought*. London: Rudolf Steiner Press, 1991.

———. *Initiation, Eternity, and the Passing Moment*. Hudson, NY: Anthroposophic Press, 1980.

———. *Karmic Relationships: Esoteric Studies,* vol. 1. London: Rudolf Steiner Press, 2012.

———. *Karmic Relationships: Esoteric Studies,* vol. 6. London: Rudolf Steiner Press, 2009.

———. *The Mission of the Folk-Souls in Relation to Teutonic Mythology*. London: Rudolf Steiner Press, 2005.

———. *An Outline of Esoteric Science*. Hudson, NY: Anthroposophic Press, 1997.

———. *Secrets of the Threshold*. Great Barrington, MA: SteinerBooks, 2007.

———. *Weltenwunder, Seelenprüfungen und Geistesoffenbarungen*. Lecture, Aug. 27, 1911 (CW 129).

von Gleich, Sigismund. *Die Wahrheit als Gesamtumfang aller Weltansichten*. Stuttgart, 1989.

Wilde, Oscar. *The Complete Letters of Oscar Wilde* (Holland, Merlin, and Rupert Hart-Davis, eds.). London: Fourth Estate, 2000.

———. "De Profundis." *Complete Works of Oscar Wilde* [1948] (J. B. Foreman, ed.). London: Collins, 1966.

www.ingramcontent.com/pod-product-compliance
Lightning Source LLC
Chambersburg PA
CBHW020935090426
42736CB00010B/1145